T HANDBOOK FOR

FOR

We the People

A Primer on Strict Construction of the Constitution

BOB HILLIARD

The Handbook for We the People:
A primer on Strict Construction of the Constitution
©2016 Bobby Hilliard

First Edition
Printed in the United States of America

Editor: Martha Hayes
Cover Designer: Derek Murphy
Layout Formatter: Jake Muelle

ISBN-10: 0-69266-608-1
ISBN-13: 978-0-69266-608-1

Contact information: foodservice@windstream.net

Website: www.wethepeoplehandbook.com

CONTENTS

Chapter 1

INTRODUCTION

Inside you will learn what has not been taught in many public schools, colleges, or law schools since the first part of the 20th Century.

If you make a reasonable effort to obtain a working knowledge of the Constitution, you will challenge questionable federal regulations while gaining a new perspective on current events when they are presented in the media. You will be able to test the constitutional literacy of new candidates and legislators alike when the need arises.

This citizen handbook uses the same original definitions and resources the founders used. It clears up generations of misinformation about our Constitution and our founders' intentions when our Constitution was created and ratified. The men who signed the Constitution, such as James Madison, Alexander Hamilton, George Washington, Thomas Jefferson, Daniel Webster, John Adams and Benjamin Franklin will be referred to in the remainder of this book as the "founders" or the "framers."

Strict construction study of the Constitution is void of opinion on the function and scope of our federal government. This is a study of the fixed principles that are embedded in the Constitution as the founders intended by the use of their own words and writings.

Our founders constructed a central government based on a framework of limited subject matter which the central government could address. Most of the subject matters which Congress may address is found in Article I, Section 8, of the Constitution. All subject matter beyond that is left to the states and to the people to address. The adherence to that framework is based on the honorable character of those who we elect to represent us and on our knowledge of the limitations in the Constitution.

Since history has proven that elected individuals were just as fallible as the rest of us, the framers understood that the government would stay within their limited bounds only if citizens were educated and involved in the process. Their studies showed that the government could not run automatically and keep our best interest.

"We the People" are an integral part of the process and the maintenance of the government.

The fixed principles found in the Bible, the Declaration of Independence, and the Constitution are the rock upon which our country was built. These principles were designed to protect the natural rights of every individual citizen of this country. Local and state governments, which are more responsive to the will of the people, have an equal duty to secure these natural rights.

When the federal government does not stay within the limits outlined in the Constitution, the founders recommended several remedies in The Federalist Papers. Amendments have been sought by some as the best remedy, but not one founder recommended more amendments as a cure to keep mischievous or fallible politicians within the guidelines provided in the Constitution. We have twenty-seven amendments, and none have stopped federal encroachments. In fact, just the opposite has happened.

Chapter 2

BASICS

American Constitutional History in a Nutshell

The Americans set up a provisional government during the war for independence. The rules for the central government were laid out in the first constitution, called the Articles of Confederation. Those rules soon proved inadequate, so the states called a convention in order to propose amendments to it. Instead of amending it during the convention, though, they ignored the rules, rejected the Articles of Confederation, and replaced it with the Constitution we have today.

This new pact created by the federation of states formed a stronger, but limited, central government by creating a Constitution of enumerated powers. If a subject is not listed by name, then the central government may not address or regulate that subject for the nation as a whole.

Many were skeptical and refused to ratify it, so James Madison, Alexander Hamilton, and John Jay wrote a series of 85 essays called The Federalist Papers in order to explain and induce the reluctant member states at the convention to ratify the Constitution. Since those papers did that, they are considered the most authoritative commentary on meanings in the Constitution. Still, some were skeptical and insisted on amendments to clarify meanings. Thus the first ten amendments were added.

Rights

The cornerstone of the Constitution depends on the proper understanding of natural rights belonging to every human being. Those natural rights are protected by restricting the scope of the central government. The framers of the Constitution limited the scope of the central government by limiting the subjects the newly designed government could address. Those subjects are listed in Article I, Section 8, of the Constitution for the most part.

The future of this country, as the founders intended, and the future of its citizens depends on an acknowledgment of the source of every citizen's individual rights. There are several different views regarding individual rights to consider:

The Declaration of Independence affirms the founder's belief that our rights come from God. Since they come from God, man was endowed with these rights long before this country was established and a written constitution was ratified. Therefore rights do not come from the Constitution, nor do they come from any amendment to the Constitution because natural rights already existed. Because the Declaration of Independence identifies the Creator as the grantor of rights, we look to the Bible, or Natural Law, to see how our founders viewed natural rights.

The Bible, or the Natural Law, reveals many natural rights:

- The right to inherit.
- To earn and keep property.
- The right to life.
- The right of self-defense.
- The right and duty to expect the civil authorities obey the law.
- The right to speak against the civil government.
- The right to live free from interference by civil government.
- The right to parent, or not become a parent.
- The right to worship, or not worship.

- The right to a fair trial.
- The right to invent.
- The right to personal privacy.
- And many more.

A key part of the philosophies the framers studied were taken from such philosophers as Marcus Cicero, John Locke, and Charles Montesquieu, along with English jurist, Sir William Blackstone. According to Locke, one distinguishing characteristics of natural rights is they can be held and enjoyed at no expense or loss to someone else's natural rights.

This is exactly the opposite of the country our forefathers had left behind. At the time, England believed in the doctrine which said kings and queens have a God-given right to rule, and rebellion against them is a sin.

One of the foundations of our political system is the belief that the government exists to serve the will of the people, and the people are the source of all political power enjoyed by the government. This is the central tenant of a republican form of government. The people can choose to give or withhold this power. This is known as the social contract theory of citizenship.

Later, John Locke expanded on the same idea by emphasizing the role of the individual. He also believed resistance to a coercive government was not just a right, but an obligation if the state abused their given power. These ideas had a huge impact on the founders, especially Thomas Jefferson and James Madison. They embedded these ideas into the Declaration of Independence when it was written:

> "...That whenever any Form of Government becomes
> destructive of these ends, it is the Right of the People to
> alter or to abolish it, and to institute new Government..."

Let us examine other views.

Many believe that rights come from the first ten amendments to the Constitution. They speak of such things as constitutional rights, the

Bill of Rights, fundamental rights, the First Amendment right to free speech, the Second Amendment right to bear arms and etc.

Natural, or unalienable, rights are the highest form of rights known as they are given by God and cannot be taken away by man. Constitutional rights are a much lower form of rights. When we say our rights come from the Constitution, we are agreeing to the submission of our rights to federal judges because Article III, Section 2, clause 1, says the judicial power shall extend to all cases "arising under this Constitution." If rights come from the first ten amendments or elsewhere in the Constitution, then they arise under the Constitution.

When judges, who the founders knew to be fallible men, have the power to determine the existence or the extent of individual rights, those rights are no longer unalienable.

Why did our founders add the Bill of Rights if those rights were such a bad idea?

There was controversy over this.

Alexander Hamilton warned in Federalist Paper No. 84, 10th paragraph, that a bill of rights would give a pretext for regulating our rights to those inclined to usurp powers.

> "I go further, and affirm that bills of rights, in the sense and to the extent in which they are contended for, are not only unnecessary in the proposed Constitution, but would even be dangerous. They would contain various exceptions to powers not granted; and, on this very account, would afford a colorable pretext to claim more than were granted. For why declare that things shall not be done which there is no power to do? Why, for instance, should it be said that the liberty of the press shall not be restrained, when no power is given by which restrictions may be imposed? I will not contend that such a provision would confer a regulating power; but it is evident that it

would furnish, to men disposed to usurp, a plausible pretense for claiming that power."

Was he right?

Why, for example, does the Second Amendment of the Bill of Rights say our right to bear arms shall not be infringed when there was no infringement on that subject mentioned anywhere in the Constitution? Assume for a minute that the Second Amendment did not exist. Each citizen's natural, unalienable right to defend himself by taking up arms or any other way would not be altered in any way.

The Supreme Court has used the First Amendment sometimes combined, or incorporated with the Fourteenth Amendment, to assume the state's role and regulate political speech, to ban prayers at football games, to ban nativity scenes on county courthouse lawns, and other such subjects the Constitution prohibits the federal courts from addressing in the first place for the nation as a whole.

Some delegates at the constitutional convention refused to ratify the Constitution without the Bill of Rights so they were added.

The best way to look at the first ten amendments is this: They are not the source of our rights since our rights come from God and thus transcend the Constitution. The first ten amendments are a partial list of things the federal government may not do, such as take away our guns. And some things they must do, such as give accused persons a fair trial.

Others view the source of citizen's rights is the Constitution as such rights are defined and discovered, from time to time by judges on the Supreme Court.

When federal judges are substituted for God as the source of rights, the entire concept of rights becomes perverted.

Another view is civil rights come from government. Some say a right is an entitlement to goods or services produced, or paid for, by somebody else. They speak of the right to medical care, the right to a free public school education, the right to housing, the right to food stamps, etc.

It is a contradiction in terms to speak of rights to products or services that are provided for, produced by, or paid for by other people because it undermines the natural rights of the providers or producers to their own private property, to the fruits of their own labors and to their liberty. Just as no one has the right to own another human being, no one has the right to own the fruits of another man's labor.

For example, if one claims to have the right to health care, then a doctor or other medical professional must provide that. Does the doctor have an equal, individual, or unalienable right to decide how he provides his own time, talent, and labor? Does the taxpayer have the unalienable, individual, or natural right to spend their own earnings on those products or services of their own choice? Or must they be forced to pay for services to others through taxes?

In conclusion, The Declaration of Independence acknowledges that our rights come from God. They are unalienable, and the purpose of civil government is to secure the rights which God gave us. Our rights do not come from the first ten amendments, they do not come from the Constitution as interpreted by federal judges, and they do not come from Congress. Our rights were bestowed by God, and, as such, they enjoy an elevated status. Unalienable means they cannot be transferred to anyone else. They are yours and yours alone.

The Declaration of Independence

The Declaration of Independence was our declaration to England of our intentions to become a free nation based on our Creator's rules, not on the King of England's rules. It also sets forth the principles upon which our Constitution was based. The whole purpose of civil government in the eyes of the founders as affirmed in the Declaration is to fulfill the theological purpose of securing the rights God gave us.

The Declaration of Independence begins the second paragraph by saying:

> "We hold these Truths to be self-evident, that all Men are created equal, that they are endowed by their Creator with certain unalienable Rights, that among these are Life, Liberty, and the Pursuit of Happiness.—That to secure these Rights, Governments are instituted among Men, deriving their just Powers from the Consent of the Governed..."

Therefore, the foundational principles outlined in our Declaration are:

- Our rights are unalienable and come from God, not the Constitution.
- The purpose of civil government is to protect our God-given rights.
- Civil government is legitimate only when it operates with the people's consent.
- Since the U.S. Constitution forms the central civil government, the government operates with our consent only when it obeys the Constitution.

The Constitution

The Constitution is composed of the preamble, seven articles, and the added amendments. Prior to adding the first ten amendments, the Bill of Rights, the founders added a Preamble to the Bill of Rights which made it clear that the first ten amendments applied only to the federal government. A copy of the Constitution, along with the amendments is provided in the back of the book for the reader's convenience.

The first three articles of the Constitution were arranged in order of power. The Legislative Branch was to have the most power. The Judicial Branch was to have the least. The Executive Branch was established to execute only the laws Congress was authorized to write. The articles and a brief description of their contents are as follows:

- Article I   – The enumerated powers of Congress.
- Article II   – The enumerated powers of the President.
- Article III – The enumerated powers of the Federal Courts.
- Article IV   – States' equality as members of the Union.
- Article V   – Amendments, two methods.
- Article VI   – Supremacy of the Constitution and Oaths of Office.
- Article VII – Ratification of the Constitution.

The basic function of a Constitution of enumerated powers is to restrict the power of civil government to a limited number of subjects, thus protecting the individual natural rights of every citizen. Webster's 1828 Dictionary definition number four of "Constitution" is:

> "The established form of government in a state, kingdom or country; a system of fundamental rules, principles and ordinances for the government of a state or nation. In free states, the *constitution* is paramount to the statutes or laws enacted by the legislature, limiting and controlling its power; and in the United States, the legislature is created, and its powers designated, by the *constitution*."

The founders understood that the Constitution is superior to laws enacted by the legislature when those laws are not aligned with the Constitution. The laws Congress writes must be confined within the limits of the Constitution. The Congress may address only subjects they are authorized to address.

The federal government and the state governments have different spheres of operation. The federal government is supreme only in those few and enumerated subjects delegated to it alone. For example, the federal government is authorized to make treaties. The states, by their own agreement in Article I, Section 10, are prohibited from making treaties. That means the right to make treaties belongs exclusively to the federal government. The states and the people retain supremacy in all other matters not delegated exclusively to the central government. When the federal government usurps powers retained by the states or the people, it becomes unlawful and illegitimate.

Our Constitution authorizes the federal government to protect our God-given rights in the following ways:

It is to protect our natural rights to life and liberty by:

- Authorizing military defense, Article I, Section 8, clauses 11-16.
- Authorizing laws against piracy and other felonies committed on the high seas, Article I, Section 8, clause 10.
- Protecting us from invasion, Article IV, Section 4.
- Prosecuting traitors, Article III, Section 3.
- Restrictive immigration policies, Article I, Section 9, clause 1.

It is to protect our natural property rights by:

- Regulating trade and commerce so we can produce, sell and prosper, Article I, Section 8, clause 3.
- Establishing uniform weights and measures and a money system based on gold and silver, Article I, Section 8, clause 5, along with Article I, Section 10, clause 1.
- Punishing counterfeiters, Article I, Section 8, clause 6.

- Making bankruptcy laws to permit the orderly dissolution or reorganization of debtors' estates with fair treatment of creditors, Article I, Section 8, clause 4.
- Issuing patents and copyrights to protect ownership of intellectual labors, Article I, Section 8, clause 8.

It is to protect our natural right to liberty by:

- Laws against slavery, Thirteenth Amendment.
- Providing fair trials in federal courts, Fourth, Fifth, Sixth, Seventh, and Eighth Amendments.

This is how our Constitution implements the founding principle which says the purpose of government is to protect the natural rights which God gave to every person.

The Federalist Papers

The Federalist Papers is a collection of 85 essays that were written by Alexander Hamilton, James Madison, and John Jay, published during 1787 and 1788, in order to explain the proposed Constitution to the citizens of the states and members of the convention to induce them to ratify it.

Since they did exactly that, they are considered to be the most authoritative source for the meanings in the Constitution.

The original text of the Federalist Papers (also known as *The Federalist*) was obtained from the Library of Congress. For the reader's convenience when paragraph numbers are quoted, they will originate from this source.

These papers give strict construction guidance to the serious student as to the founders' intent. For example, consider this question: When is a law not a law?

Hamilton answers this question in two separate papers: Federalist Paper No. 33 and Federalist Paper No. 78. A law is not a law when Congress passes laws on subjects not authorized in the Constitution.

Hamilton states in the next to the last paragraph of Federalist Paper No. 33 that when Congress makes a law which the Constitution does not authorize it to make, then it would not be the supreme law of the land, but a usurpation of power not granted by the Constitution.

Later, in Federalist Paper No. 78, 11th paragraph, he further states:

> "There is no position which depends on clearer principles, than that every act of a delegated authority, contrary to the tenor of the commission under which it is exercised, is void. No legislative act, therefore, contrary to the Constitution, can be valid."

The Federalist Papers were considered by our framers to be so authoritative that, on March 4, 1825, the minutes of the Board of Visitors of the University of Virginia with Thomas Jefferson and James Madison present voted to make The Federalist Papers one of the text books for the Law School. Pages 82 and 83 of the minutes said:

> "Resolved that it is the opinion of this board that as to... the distinctive principles of the government of our own State, and of that of the US. the best guides are to be found in
>
> 1. The Declaration of Independence, as the fundamental act of union of these States.
>
> 2. The book known by the title of 'The Federalist', being an authority to which appeal is habitually made by all, and rarely declined or denied by any as evidence of the general opinion of those who framed, and of those who accepted the Constitution of the US. on questions as to its genuine meaning.
>
> 3. The Resolutions of the General assembly of Virginia in 1799 on the subject of the Alien and Sedition laws, which appeared to accord with the predominant sense of the people of the US.
>
> 4. The Valedictory address of President Washington, as conveying political lessons of peculiar value, and that in the branch of the school of Law, which is to treat on the subject of Civil polity, these shall be used as the text and documents of the school."

By reading the founders' own words in The Federalist Papers about meanings in the Constitution, we do not have to rely on the opinions of others.

Webster's 1828 Dictionary

The earliest published dictionary we have as an aid for understanding the founders' intent is *An American Dictionary of The English Language* by Noah Webster, hereinafter referred to as Webster's 1828 Dictionary. Since word meanings can change drastically throughout time, if we are to understand the objective meaning of the Constitution, we must understand the words the same way the founders understood them. The following are a few examples of how word meanings have changed over the years: *nice* meant precise, or exact; *gay* meant jovial, or merry; *magazine* was the place to store arms and ammunition; and *color* meant "appearance to the mind."

The term *welfare* as used in the Preamble and in Article I, Section 8, clause 1, of the Constitution was defined by Webster's 1828 Dictionary, second definition, as,

> "Exemption from any unusual evil or calamity; the enjoyment of peace and prosperity, or the ordinary blessings of society and civil government."

It did not mean dependent on public relief as described in a later dictionary, *The American Heritage Dictionary of the English Language*, 1969.

Another example is the word *federal* to describe our form of government. Webster's 1828 dictionary, second definition, says,

> "Consisting in a compact between parties, particularly and chiefly between states or nations; founded on alliance by contract or mutual agreement; as a *federal* government, such as that of the United States."

However, the second definition in the current *Merriam's Dictionary* illustrates a difference in definition:

> "*a*: formed by a compact between political units that surrender their individual sovereignty to a central authority but retain limited residuary powers of government.
>
> *b*: of or constituting a form of government in which power is distributed between a central authority and a number of constituent territorial units.
>
> *c*: of or relating to the central government of a federation as distinguished from the governments of the constituent units."

Not one founder understood their agreement to form a central government to be a surrender of their individual state sovereignty.

James Madison made the distinction between a federal and a national government in Federalist Paper No. 39, 15th paragraph:

> "But if the government be national with regard to the OPERATION of its powers, it changes its aspect again when we contemplate it in relation to the EXTENT of its powers. The idea of a national government involves in it, not only an authority over the individual citizens, but an indefinite supremacy over all persons and things, so far as they are objects of lawful government. Among a people consolidated into one nation, this supremacy is completely vested in the national legislature. Among communities united for particular purposes, it is vested partly in the general and partly in the municipal legislatures. In the former case, all local authorities are subordinate to the supreme; and may be controlled, directed, or abolished by it at pleasure. In the latter, the local or municipal authorities form distinct and independent portions of the supremacy, no more subject, within their respective spheres, to the general authority, than the general authority is subject to them, within its own sphere. In this relation, then, the proposed government cannot be deemed a NATIONAL one; since its jurisdiction extends to certain

enumerated objects only, and leaves to the several States a residuary and inviolable sovereignty over all other objects."

How should we understand the Constitution? Should we understand it in the same way as our founders? Or does its meaning evolve throughout time so it means whatever group in power, at any point in time, says it means?

One side, the strict constructionists, says the Constitution has a fixed meaning, and we must look at the original intent of the Constitution.

The other side says the Constitution has no fixed meaning. They say it is an evolving, living, breathing thing which means whatever the judges, from time to time, say it means.

How do ordinary citizens learn what the judges say the Constitution means? We have to go to law school, learn how to do legal research, how to read judicial writing, and how to construe conflicting court opinions. Then we usually end up using the court's latest opinion, once we have located it, knowing it may change when a new set of judges are on the bench.

Under the second view, we do not have a constitutional government. Instead, the judiciary, the Congress, and the executive branch are free to impose their decisions on the citizens. This transforms a country from a stable fixed state where the citizens are governed by the constitution and laws, into a fluid state, where the citizens are governed by the decisions of elected and appointed political officials.

The Concept of Federalism

The concept of federalism, as the founders intended when they designed the Constitution, was one which embraced the elevated status of the states over the central or national government by virtue of limiting the number of subjects the central government may address. At the same time, state limitations are few by their own agreement in Article I, Section 10.

At the top of authority hierarchy are the people; the everyday citizens who are not subject in any way to any clause in the Constitution. Accordingly, the lines of authority rest first in the people, second in local governments, then the state governments, and last in the federal government.

Federalism is a system based on the personal integrity and virtue of those elected by the people. Without the integrity and virtue of those elected, the system fails.

Republican versus Democratic Forms of Government

A Republic, as defined by Webster's 1828 Dictionary is:

> "A commonwealth; a state in which the exercise of the sovereign power is lodged in representatives elected by the people. In modern usage, it differs from a democracy or democratic state, in which the people exercise the powers of sovereignty in person."

A constitutional republic is one in which the representatives and other officials are limited and restricted by a constitution. Our country was established as a constitutional republic, not a democracy. Those who refer to our chosen form of government as a democracy are incorrect.

A Democracy, as defined by Webster's 1828 Dictionary is:

> "Government by the people; a form of government, in which the supreme power is lodged in the hands of the people collectively, or in which the people exercise the powers of legislation. Such was the government of Athens."

The founders had a choice. They could have set up a democracy, but the founders were ardent students of history and their studies demonstrated that democracies have not succeeded to the extent in which republican forms of governments have for the benefit of the ordinary citizen. A democracy becomes inefficient as the population grows, and is mainly used in smaller forms of governments, like the family unit. Our republic, on the other hand, governs through elected representatives and could be expanded indefinitely as territories became states, with the states retaining all sovereignty unless prohibited in the Constitution by their own agreement as presented in Article I, Section 10.

A democracy exists where the majority rules; where it is possible for fifty-one percent of the people to decide what the other forty-nine percent must abide by.

A democracy has been said to be something more than two wolves and a sheep voting on what to have for dinner by James Bovard, author of *Lost Rights: The Destruction of American Liberty* (1994), p. 333.

That is not what was set up by the founders. The founders set up a central government which maximized their definition of natural liberty based on religious principles. The classic view on which our framers built was that liberty means the condition of mankind which exists only with a civil government of limited and defined powers such as the one created in our federal Constitution of 1787.

In a free country, government is decentralized. Various kinds of governmental organizations exist, each with their own sphere of operation. There are also organizations outside the government, such as religious groups, charity operations, professional, trade, and sports associations. In earlier times, these groups and associations, along with the people themselves, set the standards and handled the discipline for their members.

Webster's 1828 Dictionary lists these three types of governments, among others:

1. "Control; restraint. Men are apt to neglect the *government* of their temper and passions."

    This is the definition of self-government, or man's control and restraint over his own temper, passions, and social actions.

2. "The exercise of authority; direction and restraint exercised over the actions of men in communities, societies or states; the administration of public affairs, according to established constitution, laws and usages, or by arbitrary edicts. Prussia rose to importance under the *government* of Frederick II."

This is the definition of civil government which establishes the rules and principles by which a nation, state, county, parish, or city is governed.

3. "The exercise of authority by a parent or householder. Children are often ruined by a neglect of *government* in parents."

   This defines the family unit which assumes parents' authority over their children and other family matters.

In a totalitarian country, the civil government eliminates the other forms of government so its power is unchallenged in all spheres of life.

Consider the following examples of current government activity:

1. Self-government is being eliminated by replacing personal responsibility with tax payer funded programs through the federal government. A good example is the Social Security and Medicare programs. Those who work are forced to contribute a portion of their earnings which go to fund retirement, disability, and medical programs. In the past, matters such as retirement and medical care were considered to be individual and family responsibilities.

   Up until 1913, not one citizen was required by the government to contribute any of their personal earnings to fund a national government program. If any citizen needed help, the central government was not involved. Citizens relied on themselves along with family members, neighbors, friends, businesses, churches, professional associations, or charities.

   There was a sense of individual pride and moral responsibility in helping others. There was gratitude on the part of those receiving the help.

   There are currently many agencies, federal and state, set up to assume and replace the individual function. Government is now substituted for family, friends, or charities.

2. Family government is being eliminated by the national government by lending money to the states with no constitutional authority to do so. There is no article, section, or clause in the Constitution which grants power to the federal government to lend money to the states. In return for the federal money, the federal government has insisted on rules in regards to discipline, feeding and education of children, and reproductive health care without parental involvement.

Family government is being destroyed by the welfare and public education system. Families were meant to be the basic unit of society. Now government is assuming that role.

Matters that were treated as family responsibilities in the past, such as financial and other assistance to family members, education of children, care of aging parents, etc., have been taken over by government. We no longer look to our families for assistance. We look to the government.

3. Churches used to be considered as the moral authorities in our country, but the national government has eliminated that moral authority. Some pastors dare not speak out against the government for fear of losing their tax-exempt status. We have been deprived of the benefit of their moral guidance on issues that affect our country. The churches are restricted to speaking about saving souls, escape or rescue from this earth, what happens when we die, and other such matters that do not deal with moral integrity.

4. Charity is the work of individuals, churches, businesses, and private associations. The Bible is loaded with examples. Some private associations, such as The Salvation Army, provide Christian instruction along with assistance. Many church organizations provide hospitals for charitable purposes, but a totalitarian government will speak of reducing the tax deduction for charitable giving. As economic conditions worsen, charitable giving declines. Private charities will diminish, but the national government will always seek to expand.

5. Trades and professions have been taken over as civil governments take over more and more of the licensing and disciplining of industries such as those involving drugs, farming, nutrition, forestry, and oil exploration. The U.S. Congress even conducts unconstitutional hearings on whether sports figures take steroids.

The Oath of Office

Is the oath of office meant to be a mere formality, or did the framers include it because they considered a man's word to be a mark of integrity?

Assume you are president and Congress passes a law on the subject of "marriage," for example, and call it the Defense of Marriage Act. As president, you know marriage is not a subject in which Congress has the constitutional authority to address for the nation at a whole so you veto it. Congress overrides your veto, and it becomes a law. Are you required to enforce it?

No. It is one of the checks which the president has on the other two branches if they decide to violate the Constitution.

President's oath from Article II, Section 1, last paragraph, reads:

> "I do solemnly swear (or affirm) that I will faithfully execute the Office of President of the United States and will to the best of my Ability, preserve, protect and defend the Constitution of the United States."

Therefore it is a president's sworn duty to refuse to enforce any unconstitutional law made by Congress. Contrary to what is taught in some law schools, judges are not the only ones who have the authority to declare acts of Congress unconstitutional.

Likewise, the states and judges of the federal and state courts have the right and duty to overrule unconstitutional laws made by Congress.

Here is their oath from Article VI, clause 3:

> "The Senators and Representatives before mentioned, and the Members of the several State Legislatures, and

all executive and judicial Officers, both of the United States and of the several States, shall be bound by Oath or Affirmation, to support this Constitution; but no religious Test shall ever be required as a Qualification to any Office or public Trust under the United States."

It is a fundamental, though long suppressed, principle of our country's founding that an unconstitutional law is no law at all. It is a mere usurpation, and deserves to be treated as such.

Consider what Hamilton said in Federalist Paper No. 33, 7th paragraph:

"But it will not follow from this doctrine that acts of the large society which are NOT PURSUANT to its constitutional powers, but which are invasions of the residuary authorities of the smaller societies, will become the supreme law of the land. These will be merely acts of usurpation, and will deserve to be treated as such."

Our framers placed oaths of office in the Constitution to be a formal expression of commitment. When honored, these oaths function as checks on the powers of the federal government.

At the federal level, every member of the three branches of the government is required to take the oath of office. Thus members of each branch are required by oath to ensure the other two branch members adhere to the limits in the Constitution.

The states officials, such as state senators, state representatives, also take the oath of office, have the same check on all three branches of the federal government.

The key is this: The oath is pledged to the Constitution.

- It is not a pledge to go along with Congress.
- It is not a pledge to obey the Executive Branch.
- It is not a pledge to go along with a party's leadership decisions.
- It is not a pledge to submit to federal judges.

Nor is it to "vote their conscience" as so many Congressmen like to say. Nor do Congressmen take an oath to make the voters happy.

The oath pledges allegiance to abide by the limitations prescribed in the Constitution.

Here's another example of the president's check on Congress and Federal Courts:

Imagine you are President of the United States. Congress makes a law which says Jews must wear a yellow star on their arm, and Christians must wear a white cross, and it is a felony if they fail to wear the armbands or the crosses. You vetoed the bill, but Congress overrode your veto. A case on this subject is brought up in a federal court and is upheld by those judges. Are you going to enforce that law?

Look at your oath of office. Does your oath require you to obey Congress unless and until a majority of Supreme Court judges say you do not have to?

Even if a majority sides with Congress, will you allow U.S. Attorneys to prosecute Christians and Jews who do not wear the arm bands?

You may agree with the law, but as president, you are to defend the Constitution. You are not to defend whatever law a majority of people in Congress pass and the Supreme Court upholds.

Article II, Section 3, says the president "shall take Care that the Laws be faithfully executed." Recall the founders' intent with Hamilton's words in Federalist Paper No. 78, 11th paragraph:

> "There is no position which depends on clearer principles, than that every act of a delegated authority, contrary to the tenor of the commission under which it is exercised, is void. No legislative act, therefore, contrary to the Constitution, can be valid."

You, as president, will review Article I, Section 8, clauses 1-16, and you will ask, "Where is Congress authorized to make a law which requires Christians and Jews to wear armbands?" You will see the Constitution does not authorize Congress to make the law, and you will see the Supreme Court's opinion which upholds it is unconstitutional. You will denounce the law and the judges' opinions as mere usurpations, and you will instruct the Attorney General and U.S. Attorneys not to prosecute violations of that law.

The oath of office, Article VI, last clause, requires judges to strike down laws made by Congress which are unconstitutional.

Hamilton recognizes in Federalist Paper No. 78, 10th paragraph, et seq., that judges have the power to strike down unconstitutional laws:

> "Some perplexity respecting the rights of the courts to pronounce legislative acts void, because contrary to the Constitution, has arisen from an imagination that the doctrine would imply a superiority of the judiciary to the legislative power. It is urged that the authority which can declare the acts of another void, must necessarily be superior to the one whose acts may be declared void. As this doctrine is of great importance in all the American constitutions, a brief discussion of the ground on which it rests cannot be unacceptable."

Hamilton goes on to explain the point in later paragraphs, but some law schools still teach that federal court opinions are final, that they are the "law of the land", and once decided, there is no other recourse.

This is not the case. Federal judges are morally and intellectually fallible people, who, as our framers observed, can cause dreadful harm to our country if not guided by some moral restraint. This is why it is a mistake to assume court opinions are automatically considered the law of the land.

Thus they are subject to the moral implications of the oath for their usurpations, plus the normal recourses authorized by the Constitution on Congress, the Executive Branch, the individual states, and the people.

Reading Accuracy

Reading original source material as the founders intended is a challenge to those unfamiliar with the language of the time. One of the challenges is to understand the value the founders placed on every word. Included below are several reading challenges to help the reader:

1. The Declaration says all men are endowed by their creator with certain unalienable rights and among these rights are life, liberty and the pursuit of happiness.

   If "among these" unalienable rights are life, liberty and the pursuit of happiness, there must be others. It does not say they are the only ones. That is covered in the next chapter.

2. This example illustrates how some parts of the Constitution have been read to mean something it does not say.

   Article II, Section 2, paragraph 2, states that the president shall:

   > "...have Power, by and with the Advice and Consent of the Senate, to make Treaties, provided two thirds of the Senators present concur; and he shall nominate, and by and with the Advice and Consent of the Senate, shall appoint Ambassadors, other public Ministers and Consuls, Judges of the supreme Court, and all other Officers of the United States, whose Appointments are not herein otherwise provided for, and which shall be established by Law: but the Congress may by Law vest the Appointment of such inferior Officers, as they think proper, in the President alone, in the Courts of Law, or in the Heads of Departments."

This section provides the authority of the president to appoint his own cabinet members, subject to the consent of two-thirds of the senate members, including any vacancies that might happen during a normal session. If the president and the senate come to an agreement, the vacancy gets filled. If they cannot, it does not get filled. When the next session begins, the process starts all over again.

During the course of the year, the senate and the House of Representatives will schedule at least one recess period, most often during the July/August time period. Since there is not a provision in the above clause to provide for any vacancy that might occur during a recess, the framers added the next paragraph, Article II, Section 2, paragraph 3, to cover that contingency:

> "The President shall have Power to fill up all Vacancies that may happen during the Recess of the Senate, by granting Commissions which shall expire at the End of their next Session."

On the occasions when the president and the senate cannot agree on a replacement of the president's choice during a regular session, some presidents wait for the senate to go on recess to make the appointment of their choice by citing the above paragraph 3 as the authority to do so. But is that what this clause authorizes? No, it is not.

Using a proper reading of paragraph 3, the only constitutional appointment by the president without senate consent would be one which filled a vacancy that happened during a recess, not one that happened during a regular session. The dates of the recess are of no consequence here. The overriding issue is when the vacancy happened, not when the recess started.

3. Does the Constitution say the president is to be the Commander in Chief of the Army, Navy, and State militia forces during the time when he is president or is there a condition?

Article II, Section 2 says:

"The President shall be Commander in Chief of the Army and Navy of the United States, and of the Militia of the several States, when called into actual Service of the United States..."

That Article states he shall be the Commander in Chief only when the armed forces are "called" into actual service. Who does the calling, and how is the call implemented? Only Congress may do so as provided in Article I, Section 8, clause 11, by a declaration of war. Accordingly, he is Commander in Chief only after Congress makes a declaration of war.

4. How many times has it been said that a certain law or Supreme Court opinion is the law of the land so we must comply or we will be in violation of the law? That reference is to the second clause in Article VI of the Constitution, commonly referred to as the Supremacy Clause.

"This Constitution, and the Laws of the United States which shall be made in Pursuance thereof; and all Treaties made, or which shall be made, under the Authority of the United States, shall be the supreme Law of the Land; and the Judges in every State shall be bound thereby, any Thing in the Constitution or Laws of any State to the Contrary notwithstanding."

Note that laws are supreme only if they are made in "pursuance" of the Constitution. The Constitution limits the subjects on which Congress may create laws. Therefore, if laws are made on subjects not listed in the Constitution, they are not considered supreme. Alexander Hamilton confirmed this in Federalist Paper No. 33, 7th paragraph:

"But it will not follow from this doctrine that acts of the large society which are NOT PURSUANT to its constitutional powers, but which are invasions of the residuary authorities of the smaller societies, will become the supreme law of the land. These will be merely acts of usurpation, and will deserve to be treated as such."

Supreme Court opinions are not law. They are opinions on the cases that are, rightly or wrongly, before the Court. The only federal law in this land is the Constitution, laws made by Congress which are permitted by the Constitution, and treaties made by the president and the senate which are permitted by the Constitution.

Related Questions and Research Assignments

1. Paraphrase the following segment of Alexander Hamilton's Federalist Paper No. 33:

> "But it is said that the laws of the Union are to be the SUPREME LAW of the land. But what inference can be drawn from this, or what would they amount to, if they were not to be supreme? It is evident they would amount to nothing. A LAW, by the very meaning of the term, includes supremacy. It is a rule which those to whom it is prescribed are bound to observe. This results from every political association. If individuals enter into a state of society, the laws of that society must be the supreme regulator of their conduct. If a number of political societies enter into a larger political society, the laws which the latter may enact, pursuant to the powers intrusted to it by its constitution, must necessarily be supreme over those societies, and the individuals of whom they are composed. It would otherwise be a mere treaty, dependent on the good faith of the parties, and not a goverment, which is only another word for POLITICAL POWER AND SUPREMACY. But it will not follow from this doctrine that acts of the large society which are NOT PURSUANT to its constitutional powers, but which are invasions of the residuary authorities of the smaller societies, will become the supreme law of the land. These will be merely acts of usurpation, and will deserve to be treated as such. Hence we perceive that the clause which declares the supremacy of the laws of the Union, like the one we have just before considered, only declares a truth, which flows immediately and necessarily from the institution of a federal government. It will not, I presume, have escaped observation, that it EXPRESSLY confines this supremacy to laws made PURSUANT TO THE

CONSTITUTION; which I mention merely as an instance of caution in the convention; since that limitation would have been to be understood, though it had not been expressed."

2. Read Article I of the Constitution, including the Preamble, shown in the reference section of this book.

3. Paraphrase the following segment of Alexander Hamilton's Federalist Paper No. 22:

> "It has not a little contributed to the infirmities of the existing federal system, that it never had a ratification by the PEOPLE. Resting on no better foundation than the consent of the several legislatures, it has been exposed to frequent and intricate questions concerning the validity of its powers, and has, in some instances, given birth to the enormous doctrine of a right of legislative repeal. Owing its ratification to the law of a State, it has been contended that the same authority might repeal the law by which it was ratified. However gross a heresy it may be to maintain that a PARTY to a COMPACT has a right to revoke that COMPACT, the doctrine itself has had respectable advocates. The possibility of a question of this nature proves the necessity of laying the foundations of our national government deeper than in the mere sanction of delegated authority. The fabric of American empire ought to rest on the solid basis of THE CONSENT OF THE PEOPLE. The streams of national power ought to flow immediately from that pure, original fountain of all legitimate authority."

4. Research: With a highlighter, mark the references to God in the Declaration of Independence. See if you can find four of them in the complete document.

5. What is the basic purpose of our Constitution? Are our elected officials today upholding those purposes? Why or why not?

6. Why is it important to base our understanding of the Constitution on the Federalist Papers?

7. If Congress passes a law and the Supreme Court upholds it in court, did the founders say it was the Supreme Law of the Land? Why or why not? Name an original source for your answer.

8. Is it correct to state that we have constitutional rights? Why or why not? Name several natural rights that every single human has. Remember that a natural right cannot violate the natural rights of another.

9. In what way can amendments become dangerous to our natural rights?

10. If we have a right to a good education, give an example how that would affect the natural rights of someone else.

Chapter 3

ENUMERATED POWERS OF CONGRESS

This chapter discusses the unique concept of enumerated powers as opposed to general powers and defines the powers that are specifically delegated to the legislative branch of the federal government. The other two branches will be addressed in the following chapters as the powers of the other two branches are likewise strictly limited and enumerated. In addition, the three most violated clauses are addressed in this chapter.

The idea of a limited government revolves around the foundational structure of enumerated powers. One of the unique features of enumerated powers is the importance of what it does not say as well as what it does say. For example, Article I, Section 1, says Congress may create laws. However, since it does not give Congress permission to delegate the law-making authority to any other branch, then they cannot, for example, delegate legislating powers to the Environmental Protection Agency (EPA) since the EPA is an agency of the Executive Branch and not Congress. Article I, Section 1 says only Congress may originate laws.

Our Constitution of enumerated powers specifically lists the subjects Congress may address in Article I, Section 8. Additional subjects are listed in the amendments.

The absurdity of listing powers, if a general grant of powers had been intended, was pointed out by both Madison, in Federalist Paper No. 41, and Hamilton, in Federalist Paper No. 83.

The rest of the book revolves around this one feature of our Constitution.

This point is driven home in Article VI of the Constitution:

> "This Constitution, and the Laws of the United States which shall be made in Pursuance thereof; and all Treaties made, or which shall be made, under the authority of the United States, shall be the supreme Law of the Land..."

It says only the laws which are in "Pursuance" of the Constitution shall be considered the Supreme Law of the Land.

The concept of enumerated powers may be thought of as a grocery list of only those things that may be purchased. Assume that you have been asked to go to the local grocery store to buy a list of items. You were given a grocery list with twenty-one grocery items on it. In reading the list, you noticed that peanut butter is not on the list. When you get to the grocery store, you are tempted to buy a jar of peanut butter because you know your family members will love it. However, since it is not on the list, you cannot buy it even if the purchase would benefit your relationship with your family. You also cannot stop and visit a friend along the way. You were given specific permission only to buy. Visiting was not one of the listed tasks you were given permission to do. In the case of our Constitution of enumerated powers, it is just as important to understand what it does not say as well as what it does say.

However, if you asked the originator of the list to amend it by adding peanut butter and he/she gave you proper permission, then it would be perfectly OK to pick up a jar, but only under that one circumstance alone. Our Constitution can be compared to the grocery list.

For example, parks (*peanut butter*, if you like) is not on the list which Congress may address, but we have national parks anyway. The Constitution leaves the subject of parks to the states, or the people to address since it is not a subject listed within the U.S. Constitution.

Thus, without an amendment giving Congress the authority to address the subject of parks, national parks are unconstitutional for the nation as a whole. On the other hand, state parks are constitutional if the states' constitutions permit it. Nothing in the U.S. Constitution prevents the states from addressing the subject of parks.

That point is confirmed by the 10th Amendment when it says:

> "The powers not delegated to the United States by the Constitution, nor prohibited by it to the States, are reserved to the States respectively, or to the people."

In that case, the subject of parks would then be considered a reserved power of the states or the People.

Another example of enumerated powers can be found in Article I, Section 8, beginning with the fifth clause. It says Congress shall have the power "To coin Money, regulate the Value thereof, and of foreign Coin, and fix the Standard of Weights and Measures..."

It gives Congress the authority only to "coin Money," but does not give them the authority to print money because it is not pointed out that they can print currency. Nor does it give Congress the authority to delegate coining or printing our national currency to any outside group as they do now with the Federal Reserve because it does not say they can. As a result, the monetary system of paper we use today is unconstitutional.

Congress is not authorized to pass any law on any subject just because a majority in Congress thinks the law is a good idea. Instead, the areas in which Congress is authorized to act for the nation as a whole are listed mostly in Article I, Section 8, and more clearly defined in the Federalist Papers. Looking at the list below, there are no subjects such as transportation, education, labor, agriculture, housing, energy, etc. They are not on the list, but Congress makes unlawful and unconstitutional laws on those subjects for the nation as a whole.

Article I, Section 8, enumerates to Congress the powers:

1. To lay certain taxes.
2. To pay the debts of the United States.

3. To declare war and make rules of warfare.
4. To raise and support armies and a navy and to make rules governing the military forces.
5. To call forth the militia for certain purposes, and to make rules governing the militia.
6. To regulate commerce with foreign nations, and among the states, and with the Indian tribes.
7. To establish uniform rules of naturalization.
8. To establish uniform laws on bankruptcies.
9. To coin money and regulate the value thereof.
10. To fix the standard of weights and measures.
11. To provide for the punishment of counterfeiting.
12. To establish post offices and post roads.
13. To issue patents and copyrights.
14. To create courts inferior to the Supreme Court.
15. To define and punish piracies and felonies committed on the high seas, and offenses against the Laws of Nations.

Other provisions of the Constitution grant Congress powers to make laws regarding:

16. An enumeration of the population for purposes of apportionment of Representatives and direct taxes in Article. I, Section 2, clause 3.
17. Elections of Senators and Representatives in Article I, Section 4, clause 1, and their pay as shown in Article I, Section 6.
18. After 1808, to prohibit importation of slaves in Article I, Section 9, clause 1.
19. A restricted power to suspend Writs of Habeas Corpus in Article I, Section 9, clause 2.
20. To revise and control imposts or duties on imports or exports which may be laid by states as shown in Article I, Section 10, clauses 2 and 3.
21. A restricted power to declare the punishment of treason in Article III, Section 3, clause 2.
22. Implementation of the Full Faith and Credit clause in Article IV, Section 1.
23. Procedures for amendments to the Constitution as described in Article V

Amendments to the Constitution grant additional powers to Congress respecting certain civil rights and voting rights, the lawfully incurred public debt, income tax, successions to vacated offices, dates of assembly, and appointment of representatives from the District of Columbia that we know as Washington D.C.

The Constitution authorizes Congress to exercise only the listed powers above.

The above list is the federal government's grocery list.

Notice the matters Congress may address (listed above) are matters which do not come up in our everyday lives.

Matters regarding the subject of automobiles are not listed, but we have unlawful federal regulations on air bags, seat belts, exhaust emissions, mileage requirements, computerized brake systems, bumpers, among many more. Therefore, federal regulations on automobile manufacturers are unconstitutional and unlawful for the nation as a whole. In fact, the whole subject of transportation, in any form, is not on the list. Thus it is off limits for the federal government to address. That also includes air, rail, and to some extent, water transportation as well. These are matters left to the states, or the people, to regulate without an amendment to the contrary.

Matters regarding the subject of consumer goods are not up there, either, but we have federal requirements which regulate the amount of water flow a faucet may have, how much water your toilet tank can hold, what type of light bulb manufacturers may produce, etc. There are thousands of such regulations, all unlawful and unconstitutional. There has not been any amendment passed which gives Congress the authority to address these subjects.

The question is not whether the regulations are good or useful, but whether Congress made the regulations without getting the proper authority to do so. For example, statistics have shown that seat belts save lives. But the overriding question asks if the federal government makes those laws without proper, lawful permission to do so, what other laws will they make? What are the limits?

A good example of how nongovernmental, free market solutions solve consumer goods quality issues is the Good Housekeeping's Seal of Approval which leaves the purchasing decisions to the individual, not to unlawful governmental regulations. Another example is the Better Business Bureau. Businesses that affiliate with the BBB and adhere to its standards do so through industry self-regulation.

Now, instead of addressing what Congress may not do, let us address their broader powers.

Two provisions of the Constitution grant to Congress broad legislative powers, but only in defined areas:

1. Article I, Section 8, next to last clause, grants to Congress exclusive legislation over the following areas: the seat of the government of the United States, not to exceed 10 square miles, forts, arsenals, dock-yards, and other needful buildings. "Exclusive" means only the U.S. Congress may make laws over the particular areas designated and those laws are not limited to the enumerated powers only. The states have no authority here if it's exclusive to the federal government.

   James Madison said in Federalist Paper No. 43 that it is necessary for the United States to have complete authority at the seat of government and over forts, magazines, and etc. established by the federal government.

   Note: Throughout this book, we add the note "for the nation as a whole" because in certain areas that are noted in Article I, Section 8, next to last clause, Congress can make laws on anything they please. But for the nation as a whole, they must adhere to the enumerated subjects alone. In many cases, it is not correct to make a blanket statement about the restricted powers of the federal government without also acknowledging the exceptions.

   As a further reminder of the art of understanding enumerated powers, notice the last part in Article I, Section 8, next to last clause where it says the federal government may exercise exclusive authority over "all Places purchased." The Constitution limits those purchases to certain uses. The land must be used for the "Erection of Forts, Magazines, Arsenals, dock-Yards and other needful Buildings" because it does not say the purchases can be used for anything else.

Recall a few years ago when the Bureau of Land Management (BLM), an agency of the Executive Branch, claimed ownership of certain property in Nevada. There was a standoff between a ranch owner and the BLM over unpaid grazing fees that developed into an armed confrontation between protesters and law enforcement. The federal agents left the scene after the confrontation. They had no lawful, constitutional authority to claim that land for the purpose of grazing.

2. Article IV, Section 3, clause 2, grants Congress power to dispose of and make all needful rules and regulations respecting the "Territory" or other property belonging to the United States. As these territories became states, Congress's powers under this article were terminated.

Thus Congress has no authority, over the country as a whole, to consider the subjects of loans, health care, labor, personal savings or retirement accounts, energy consumption, emissions, education, housing, work safety, etc.

Under the two listed exceptions above, they are authorized to make any law they want. If on an Army base, for instance, they wanted to make a law which says only vegetables may be served in the base cafeterias, that regulation would be lawful and constitutional. That is why they can lawfully regulate the subject of clothing and require uniforms for all members of the armed forces on a federal armed forces base.

However, for the nation as a whole, the laws which Congress has passed on such topics are unconstitutional when they pertain to areas outside the scope of the legislative powers granted to Congress by the Constitution.

We the People did not give such powers to Congress when we ordained and established the Constitution, created the Congress, and listed its enumerated powers. And these powers are not granted to Congress in any of the amendments.

Another way to categorize Congress's legislative powers that we granted to Congress is by category. They fall into four main categories:

1. International commerce and relations.
2. War.
3. A domestic establishment of a uniform commercial system: weights and measures, patents and copyrights, a monetary system based on gold and silver, bankruptcy law, a limited power over interstate commerce, and mail delivery. Congress also has the power to establish lower federal courts and make rules for naturalization.
4. Protection of certain civil and voting rights.

All other powers are retained by the states or the people. President Franklin D. Roosevelt (FDR) proposed New Deal programs and Congress passed them. At first, the Supreme Court ruled 5 to 4 that these programs were unconstitutional since they were outside the legislative powers granted to Congress. But when FDR proposed the Judicial Procedures Reform Bill of 1937 which threatened to rearrange the court by adding judges who he would select, one judge changed his mind, and the Court approved FDR's programs. The central provision of the bill would have granted the President power to appoint an additional justice to the U.S. Supreme Court, up to a maximum of six, for every member of the court over the age of 70 years and 6 months.

Since then, most law schools do not teach strict construction of the Constitution. Instead, they teach opinions of the Supreme Court which purport to explain why Congress has the power to regulate anything it pleases. Law schools have produced generations of lawyers and judges who believe that the below three clauses permit Congress to do whatever it wants.

General Welfare Clause

This clause is mentioned in two places: The Preamble of the Constitution and Article I, Section 8, first clause of the Constitution.

The Preamble says:

> "We the People of the United States, in Order to form a more perfect Union, establish Justice, insure domestic Tranquility, provide for the common defence, promote the general Welfare, and secure the Blessings of Liberty to ourselves and our Posterity, do ordain and establish this Constitution for the united States of America."

Article I, Section 8, first clause, says:

> "The Congress shall have the Power To lay and collect Taxes, Duties, Imposts and Excises, to pay the Debts and provide for the common Defence and general Welfare of the United States; but all Duties, Imposts and Excises shall be uniform throughout the United States."

What about the general welfare clause? Does it give Congress power to pass any law on any subject as long as it is for the general welfare of the United States?

No, it does not.

James Madison addresses this clause in Federalist Paper No. 41, 4th and 5th paragraphs.

Note: The writings of the founders are often difficult to read. To get the accurate context intended by the author, the reader is encouraged to persist and read the whole paper, not just these selected paragraphs.

In order to make it easier to read and absorb the contents of The Federalist Papers, it is best if the actual quote is presented in the beginning. Just below it, we will paraphrase what the author is saying as it applies to the particular clause. This is done for the first three segments of the paragraph, leaving the last segment for the reader.

Here is the paragraph with paraphrases below each segment of Federalist Paper No. 41 in Madison's words below.

In the first segment of paragraph 4, Madison says:

> "Some, who have not denied the necessity of the power of taxation, have grounded a very fierce attack against the Constitution, on the language in which it is defined. It has been urged and echoed, that the power 'to lay and collect taxes, duties, imposts, and excises, to pay the debts, and provide for the common defense and general welfare of the United States,' amounts to an unlimited commission to exercise every power which may be alleged to be necessary for the common defense or general welfare. No stronger proof could be given of the distress under which these writers labor for objections, than their stooping to such a misconstruction."

Madison is saying those who are opposed to ratifying the Constitution are stooping to a new low of behavior when they say the general welfare clause gives the federal government an unlimited authority to tax citizens in order to fund an unlimited array of matters. Madison, in fact, labeled that line of thinking as a "misconstruction."

In the second segment, he continues:

> "Had no other enumeration or definition of the powers of the Congress been found in the Constitution, than the general expressions just cited, the authors of the objection might have had some color for it; though it would have been difficult to find a reason for so awkward a form of describing an authority to legislate in all possible cases. A

power to destroy the freedom of the press, the trial by jury, or even to regulate the course of descents, or the forms of conveyances, must be very singularly expressed by the terms 'to raise money for the general welfare.'"

In this paragraph he explains that if there had not been a list to begin with, those who say the general welfare clause gives unlimited powers might have a point. "To raise money for the general welfare" must be an extraordinary phrase if it includes the power to destroy the freedom of the press, the trial by jury, inheritances, or other such documents. In other words, it is a pretty good stretch of his words.

In the third segment, Madison says:

"But what color can the objection have, when a specification of the objects alluded to by these general terms immediately follows, and is not even separated by a longer pause than a semicolon? If the different parts of the same instrument ought to be so expounded, as to give meaning to every part which will bear it, shall one part of the same sentence be excluded altogether from a share in the meaning; and shall the more doubtful and indefinite terms be retained in their full extent, and the clear and precise expressions be denied any signification whatsoever? For what purpose could the enumeration of particular powers be inserted, if these and all others were meant to be included in the preceding general power? Nothing is more natural nor common than first to use a general phrase, and then to explain and qualify it by a recital of particulars. But the idea of an enumeration of particulars which neither explain nor qualify the general meaning, and can have no other effect than to confound and mislead, is an absurdity, which, as we are reduced to the dilemma of charging either on the authors of the objection or on the authors of the Constitution, we must take the liberty of supposing, had not its origin with the latter."

Madison is asking the rhetorical question of how anyone can interpret this document as general legislative permission to make laws on any subject when we provided a specific list. He went further and labeled the idea to be an "absurdity."

For the fourth segment, keeping the context, the founders were trying to write a new document which would create a more useful central government because the old one, the Articles of Confederation, was unsatisfactory. They wanted to make a "more perfect union" as they said in the preamble.

Madison further reasons in this last segment, including the last paragraph:

> "The objection here is the more extraordinary, as it appears that the language used by the convention is a copy from the articles of Confederation. The objects of the Union among the States, as described in article third, are 'their common defense, security of their liberties, and mutual and general welfare.' The terms of article eighth are still more identical: 'All charges of war and all other expenses that shall be incurred for the common defense or general welfare, and allowed by the United States in Congress, shall be defrayed out of a common treasury,' etc. A similar language again occurs in article ninth. Construe either of these articles by the rules which would justify the construction put on the new Constitution, and they vest in the existing Congress a power to legislate in all cases whatsoever.

> But what would have been thought of that assembly, if, attaching themselves to these general expressions, and disregarding the specifications which ascertain and limit their import, they had exercised an unlimited power of providing for the common defense and general welfare? I appeal to the objectors themselves, whether they would in that case have employed the same reasoning in justification of Congress as they now make use of against

the convention. How difficult it is for error to escape its own condemnation!"

Madison's reasoning could be compared to the grocery list example illustrated earlier. If the person who made the list had intended for you to be able to buy just anything you wanted, there would not have been any need to list each item. What's the point of having a list at all?

Our founders understood that the general welfare, the enjoyment of peace and prosperity, the enjoyment of the ordinary blessings of society and civil government, was possible only with a civil government which was strictly limited and restricted in what it was given power to do.

We have listed only one of The Federalist Papers which addresses the general welfare clause. The other Federalist Papers that address that subject are Nos. 41, 83, 45, 39, 14, and 27.

The Commerce Clause

Does the interstate commerce clause give Congress power to pass laws on any subject which affects commerce?

No, it does not.

The clause in Article I, Section 8, clause 3, says Congress shall have the power "To regulate Commerce with foreign Nations, and among the several States, and with the Indian Tribes."

In Federalist Paper No. 22, and Federalist Paper No. 42, Alexander Hamilton and James Madison explain that the purpose of the commerce clause is to prohibit the states from imposing tolls and tariffs on articles of import and export when the merchandise is transported through the states for purposes of buying and selling. For example, if you live in South Carolina and ordered a new lamp from a shop in New York to be delivered to you, it could cost you much more than advertised, because as the lamp passed through the various states to be delivered to you, some states might be tempted to add taxes or fees. The founders believed that these added expenses on products would be a hindrance to a free economy.

As mentioned above, the fourth paragraph of Federalist Paper No. 42 says:

> "The defect of power in the existing Confederacy to regulate the commerce between its several members, is in the number of those which have been clearly pointed out by experience. To the proofs and remarks which former papers have brought into view on this subject, it may be added that without this supplemental provision, the great and essential power of regulating foreign commerce would have been incomplete and ineffectual. A very material object of this power was the relief of the States

which import and export through other States, from the improper contributions levied on them by the latter. Were these at liberty to regulate the trade between State and State, it must be foreseen that ways would be found out to load the articles of import and export, during the passage through their jurisdiction, with duties which would fall on the makers of the latter and the consumers of the former. We may be assured by past experience, that such a practice would be introduced by future contrivances; and both by that and a common knowledge of human affairs, that it would nourish unceasing animosities, and not improbably terminate in serious interruptions of the public tranquillity. To those who do not view the question through the medium of passion or of interest, the desire of the commercial States to collect, in any form, an indirect revenue from their uncommercial neighbors, must appear not less impolitic than it is unfair; since it would stimulate the injured party, by resentment as well as interest, to resort to less convenient channels for their foreign trade. But the mild voice of reason, pleading the cause of an enlarged and permanent interest, is but too often drowned, before public bodies as well as individuals, by the clamors of an impatient avidity for immediate and immoderate gain."

Federalist Paper No. 44 and Federalist Paper No. 56 have references to the same effect.

As an example of the courts willingness to declare some laws constitutional, based on this clause, consider the 1942 case of Wickard versus Filburn. It affected a farmer and his ability to grow his own crops on his own land. In this case, the court said that the commerce clause extends to local intrastate activities which affect interstate commerce, even if the activities are not commerce. The Court also asserted that Congress has the power to regulate prices of commodities and the practices which affect such prices.

That means if you have tomato plants in your back yard for use in your own kitchen, you are affecting interstate commerce and are subject to regulation by Congress. The Court's reasoning is this: If you were not growing tomatoes in your back yard, you would buy them at the market. If you were buying them at the market, some of what you bought might come from another State. So, by not buying them at the market, you are affecting interstate commerce because you did not buy something you otherwise would have bought at the market.

The Federalist Papers that address the commerce clause are Federalist Papers Nos. 22, 42, 44, and 56.

Necessary and Proper Clause

Does the necessary and proper clause in Article I, Section 8, last clause, also known as the *elastic* or *sweeping* clause, allow Congress to make any laws on any subject which the people in Congress think are necessary and proper?

No, it does not.

That clause says:

> "To make all Laws which shall be necessary and proper for carrying into Execution the foregoing Powers, and all other Powers vested by this Constitution in the Government of the United States, or in any Department or Officer thereof."

In Federalist Paper No. 33, the 2nd paragraph, Alexander Hamilton says:

> "...it may be affirmed with perfect confidence that the constitutional operation of the intended government would be precisely the same, if these clauses were entirely obliterated, as if they were repeated in every article."

Further, in the third paragraph of the same paper, he says the clause gives Congress a right to pass all laws necessary and proper for Congress to execute its *declared* powers:

> "What is a power, but the ability or faculty of doing a thing? What is the ability to do a thing, but the power of employing the MEANS necessary to its execution? What is a LEGISLATIVE power, but a power of making LAWS? What are the MEANS to execute a LEGISLATIVE power but LAWS? What is the power of laying and

> collecting taxes, but a LEGISLATIVE POWER, or a power of MAKING LAWS, to lay and collect taxes? What are the proper means of executing such a power, but NECESSARY and PROPER laws?"

He goes on in the fourth paragraph:

> "And it is EXPRESSLY to execute these powers that the sweeping clause, as it has been affectedly called, authorizes the national legislature to pass all NECESSARY and PROPER laws. If there is any thing exceptionable, it must be sought for in the specific powers upon which this general declaration is predicated. The declaration itself, though it may be chargeable with tautology or redundancy, is at least perfectly harmless."

James Madison agrees with Hamilton's explanation in Federalist Paper No. 44.

In other words, the clause permits the execution of powers already declared and granted. Hamilton and Madison make it clear that no additional substantive powers are granted by this clause.

The Federalist Papers that address that particular clause are Federalist Papers Nos. 33, 39, and 44.

Our framers insisted that Congress is restricted to its enumerated powers in more than one instance. James Madison says in Federalist Paper No. 45, 7th paragraph:

> "The powers delegated by the proposed Constitution to the federal government are few and defined. Those which are to remain in the State governments are numerous and indefinite. The former will be exercised principally on external objects, as war, peace, negotiation, and foreign commerce; with which last the power of taxation will, for the most part, be connected. The powers reserved to the several States will extend to all the objects which, in the

ordinary course of affairs, concern the lives, liberties, and properties of the people, and the internal order, improvement, and prosperity of the State."

In Federalist Paper No. 14, 8th paragraph, Madison explains:

"In the first place it is to be remembered that the general government is not to be charged with the whole power of making and administering laws. Its jurisdiction is limited to certain enumerated objects, which concern all the members of the republic, but which are not to be attained by the separate provisions of any."

Rule of Law or Rule of Man?

Does our current government operate under the rule of law or the rule of man?

What is the rule of law?

According to Merriam-Webster's online dictionary, the rule of law is defined as "a legal rule; a determination of the applicable rule as distinguished from a finding of fact" and "adherence to due process: government by law."

Accordingly, the rule of law prevails when the civil authorities act in accordance with a body of law which is established by a higher authority.

Alexander Hamilton recognized in Federalist Paper No. 33 that the federal government is our creature, and we are to judge the acts of the federal government by using the standard we have formed.

That standard is the Constitution.

The Constitution, as viewed by the founders in previous chapters, is superior to Congress.

The rule of law prevails when the people in the federal government obey the Constitution. When they act outside the enumerated powers, they abandon the rule of law. Instead, they embrace the rule of men. The rule of man is the absence of the rule of law.

With that foundation, the census is a good example in regards to what the Constitution says and what it does not say.

Article I, Section 2, clause 3, provides that an enumeration of the people shall be taken every 10 years for the purposes of apportionment of (1) direct taxes, and (2) Representatives to the House.

In Federalist Paper No. 54, last paragraph, James Madison explains the "salutary effect" of having a "common measure" for determining both the number of representatives for each state and the amount of the direct taxes each state is to pay. The accuracy of the census depends on the cooperation of the states while the "common measure" discourages the states from overstating or understating the numbers of their population.

To these ends, we gave the federal government the authority to ask only the number of persons living in our homes and whether any of us are Indians.

Now let us look at some of the questions on the 2010 census, the short form, at www.census.gov./2010census.

Question No. 3 asks whether you own your home subject to a mortgage, whether you own it free and clear, whether you pay rent, or whether you live rent free. The justification they give for asking is that the information is used "to administer housing programs and to inform planning decisions."

Is housing an enumerated subject Congress may address? No, it is not.

In question numbers 4 and 5 they ask the citizen's full name and telephone number.

In question number 6 they ask that you provide whether you are male or female. They say that they ask because "many federal programs must differentiate between males and females for funding, implementing and evaluating their programs."

In question number 7 they ask your age and date of birth. They say they "need data about age to interpret most social and economic characteristics, such as forecasting the number of people eligible for Social Security or Medicare benefits. The data are widely used in planning and evaluating government programs and policies that provide funds or services for children, working-age adults, women of childbearing age, or the older population."

In question number 8 they ask whether anyone in your home is of Hispanic, Latino, or Spanish origin.

In question number 9 they ask you to list the race of everyone in your household. The reasons they give for asking include, "to monitor racial disparities in characteristics such as health and education and to plan and obtain funds for public services."

Housing programs are not among the enumerated powers of Congress. Neither are federal programs which differentiate between males and females, Social Security programs, Medicare programs, and other government programs for children, adults, childbearing women, or older citizens.

These are just a few of the subjects in which Congress does not have any constitutional authority to address.

This distinction between the rule of law or the rule of man was illustrated in a discussion about the census questions between Megyn Kelly of Fox News Television and Congresswoman Michele Bachmann from Minnesota on June 25, 2009.

Ms. Kelly illustrated the rule of men while Representative Bachmann illustrated the rule of law.

Megyn Kelly and Michelle Bachmann both expressed disapproval of the intrusiveness of questions on the census. But Ms. Kelly brought up that a spokesperson for the Census Bureau said that the U.S. code says anyone over eighteen who refuses to answer any of the questions on the census can be fined up to $5,000 dollars.

Ms. Kelly asked Rep. Bachmann,

> "...how do you respond to those who say that, look, we've been doing it for decades since then. The law is what the law is and you as a lawmaker should know better than to break it."

Rep. Bachmann answered,

> "I'm saying for myself and for my family, our comfort level is we will comply with the Constitution. Article I, section two: we will give the number of the people in our home. And that's where we're going to draw the line."

Ms. Kelly then asked,

> "But Congresswoman, and let me just press you on this because that's what the Constitution says, OK, you've got to give the number of people in your home. But as you know, in this country we do not live just by the Constitution. We have laws that people like you passed and the US code – and I have it – says and the Census Bureau has got a point. It says that anybody whoever over eighteen years of age who refuses or willfully neglects to answer any of the questions on the schedule submitted to him in connection with the census shall be fined not more than five thousand dollars. So that's a law on the books. So why don't you try to change the law as opposed to defying the one that's already out there?"

From this example, the reader can see the federal government requires answers to questions which the Constitution does not permit them to ask in order to administer programs which the Constitution does not authorize them to administer. Then they assign fines on those who do not comply with the unconstitutional acts.

That is the rule of men.

Under the rule of law, the Constitution, federal census officials may ask no more than the number of persons residing in your home.

That was all we the people authorized them to ask at Article I, Section 2, clause 3. Hence, that is all they may lawfully ask.

When the federal government officials exceed the powers that were granted to them in the Constitution, they usurp powers and act in defiance of the law.

Alexander Hamilton, in Federalist Paper No. 16, 10th paragraph, understood that we the people are the "natural guardians of the Constitution," and he expected us to be "enlightened enough to distinguish between a legal exercise and an illegal usurpation of authority."

Federal Criminal Laws

Since the discussion so far has concentrated on what subjects the federal government may address with regard to civil laws, let us now address federal criminal laws.

What criminal laws are Congress authorized to make? Is it lawful, for example, to make it a federal crime to shorten the barrel of a shotgun?

The Constitution grants to Congress only limited powers to make criminal laws. These powers fall into five categories:

1. Those made pursuant to express authorizations for four specific crimes.
2. Those made under the necessary and proper clause.
3. Those made for the few tiny geographical areas over which Congress has exclusive legislative powers.
4. Those governing the military.
5. Those made pursuant to two of the amendments to the Constitution.

Let's look at each category.

1. Those criminal laws made pursuant to express authorizations for four specific crimes:

   Art. I, Section 8 grants to Congress authority to define and punish counterfeiting, piracies, and felonies committed on the high seas, and offenses against the "Laws of Nations." Article III, Section 3 grants to Congress a restricted power to declare the punishment of treason.

   The seventh definition under the word "law" in Webster's 1828 Dictionary defines Laws of nations as:

"Laws of nations, the rules that regulate the mutual intercourse of nations or states. These rules depend on natural *law* or the principles of justice which spring from the social state; or they are founded on customs, compacts, treaties, leagues and agreements between independent communities.

By the *law* of nations, we are to understand that code of public instruction, which defines the rights and prescribes the duties of nations, in their intercourse with each other."

One example of a law of nations based on custom is that of diplomatic immunity. From antiquity to modern times, envoys between warring armies have been entitled to safe conduct while on their missions. For example, Ramses II of Egypt and the Hittites negotiated a treaty which included provisions for the immunity of each nation's diplomats within the receiving nation. Our concept of diplomatic immunity is thus an ancient one.

2. Those criminal laws made under the necessary and proper clause:

> Article I, Section 8, last clause, grants to Congress the power "To make all Laws which shall be necessary and proper for carrying into Execution the foregoing Powers vested by this Constitution in the Government of the United States, or in any Department or Officer thereof."

This necessary and proper clause allows Congress to make criminal laws when necessary to enforce *declared* powers vested by the Constitution in the federal government.

As a result, Congress has authority under the necessary and proper clause to:

- Make criminal laws enforcing the "Taxes, Duties, Imposts and Excises" authorized by Article I, Section 8, clause1.

- Make criminal laws prohibiting the filing of false statements or claims in bankruptcy court, Article I, Section 8, clause 4.
- Make criminal laws forbidding the importation of slaves after 1808, Article I, Section 9, clause 1.
- Make criminal statues prohibiting the accepting of bribes by civil authorities of the United States. Since Article II, Section 4, mentions impeachment of civil officers for, among other things, bribery. By implication, Congress is authorized to pass laws on bribery.
- Make criminal laws declaring perjury and lying under oath in federal court. The main duty of the federal judiciary created by Article III is to conduct trials in the limited category of cases which they are permitted to hear, including parties and witnesses. Parties and witnesses must be required to tell the truth, so, it would be necessary and proper for Congress to make laws which declare perjury and lying under oath in federal court criminal offenses.

These examples are not exclusive. There are doubtless additional criminal laws which are appropriate applications of the necessary and proper clause.

Private citizens in the course of ordinary daily life would rarely, if ever, find themselves in situations where these criminal laws would apply to them.

3. Those made for the few tiny geographical areas where Congress has exclusive legislative powers:

Article I, Section 8, next to last clause, authorizes Congress to exercise exclusive legislation in all cases whatsoever over small defined geographical areas: the seat of the government of the United States, not to exceed ten squares miles, forts, dock-yards, magazines, arsenals, and other needful buildings.

As Madison said in Federalist Paper No. 43, it is necessary for the government of the United States to have "complete authority" at the seat of government and over forts, dockyards, etc. This means Congress has the authority to make a full range of laws that criminalizes murder, robbery, extortion, arson, rape, kidnapping, and all the others they do not have permission to address outside these small defined geographical areas.

In the course of their ordinary daily life, private citizens would not be affected by these criminal laws unless they are inside these same small defined geographical areas.

Article IV, Section 3, clause 2, also granted Congress authority to dispose of and make all needful rules and regulations respecting the territories belonging to the United States, such as the Western Territories before they became states. Federalist Paper No. 43, 11th paragraph, also alludes to this subject. This gave Congress authority to create full range of criminal laws to govern those territories until such time as they became states. When they became states, jurisdiction to enact criminal laws was transferred to the new state.

4. Those governing the military:

Article I, Section 8, clause 14, authorizes Congress "To make Rules for the Government and Regulation of the land and naval Forces." Under this grant of authority, Congress has properly enacted The Uniform Code of Military Justice. This is the criminal code which governs members of our military forces. This covers all the standard criminal offenses plus additional crimes which are appropriate to those in the military such as the failure to obey a lawful order, dereliction of duty, absent without leave, desertion, conduct unbecoming an officer, etc.

Civilians are not affected by the criminal code which governs our military forces.

5. Those made pursuant to two of the amendments to the Constitution:

- The 13th Amendment would authorize Congress to make criminal laws punish those who keep slaves.
- The 16th Amendment authorizes Congress to make criminal laws to enforce the income tax.
- The 18th Amendment, now repealed, authorized Congress and the states to make laws which punish those who manufacture or traffic intoxicating liquors.

Thus Congress's criminal jurisdiction over private citizens under all amendments is limited to those who keep slaves or do not pay income taxes.

Much of the present federal criminal code is not lawful because the laws which are contained in it are outside the legislative powers granted to Congress by the Constitution. Congress has no general authority to pass criminal laws beyond those areas where they have exclusive authority, such as members of the military and those areas listed in Article I, Section 8, clause 17, which include: Washington D.C. "Forts, Magazines, Arsenals, dock-Yards and other needful Buildings."

Federal laws purported to be of general application throughout the several states which criminalize acts in respect to firearms, ammunition, hate crimes, environmental crimes, economic crimes, banking crimes, computer crimes, murder, kidnapping, narcotics, arson, extortion, and so forth are all unconstitutional usurpations.

As a result, the federal prisons are filled with inmates convicted under laws which are not authorized by the Constitution.

Do we have a remedy for these usurpations by Congress? Madison says in Federalist Paper No.44:

> "In the first instance, the success of the usurpation will depend on the executive and judiciary departments, which are to expound and give effect to the legislative acts; and in the last resort a remedy must be obtained

from the people who can, by the election of more faithful representatives, annul the acts of the usurpers."

When Congress creates a criminal law for which it lacks constitutional authority, the Executive Branch, in the person of the U.S. Attorney, has the power and duty to refuse to prosecute the violation.

If that check fails, the Judicial Branch has the power to declare the statute unconstitutional. It is the responsibility of defense counsel to raise the issue of the constitutionality of the statute under which defendant is charged.

But many lawyers, like a lot of others in our modern culture, are often unaware that Congress must be authorized by the Constitution to enact a criminal law before the law is valid. The judge has an independent responsibility to raise the issue of the constitutionality of the statute. But like some defense counsels and others, many judges often do not know that Congress must have constitutional authority for their acts.

If the U.S. attorneys and federal judges both fail in their obligations to enforce the Constitution, Madison said the last option was up to the people to elect "more faithful representatives."

Hamilton said in Federalist Paper No. 33, 6th paragraph:

> "If the federal government should overpass the just bounds of its authority and make a tyrannical use of its powers, the people, whose creature it is, must appeal to the standard they have formed, and take such measures to redress the injury done to the Constitution as the exigency may suggest and prudence justify."

The standard we have formed is the Constitution.

Hamilton said that when our "creature," the federal government, usurps power, we the people are to judge the conduct by the standard of the Constitution, and we are to take appropriate action to "redress the injury done to the Constitution" including:

- Demands for impeachment.
- Recall petitions.
- Defeating oath-breaking representatives in the next election.
- Nullification by states.
- Jury nullification.
- Non-violent civil disobedience.
- Ignoring unconstitutional laws.

Recall that Hamilton stated in Federalist Paper No. 16, 10th paragraph, that for "an illegal usurpation of authority" to be successful "would require not merely a factious majority in the legislature, but the concurrence of the courts of justice and of the body of the people."

Hamilton contemplated in Federalist Paper No. 23, next to last paragraph, "the most vigilant and careful attention of the people."

Thus the people, as the natural guardians of the Constitution, have a duty to protest when the authorities act without proper constitutional authority.

Did the framers of the Constitution advocate anarchy? No. The state legislatures have whatever authority that was granted to them by their state Constitutions to enact criminal codes applicable to those within the borders of their states.

Federal Budget

How do enumerated powers affect the federal budget?

The U.S. Constitution does not provide for a budget because a budget is not needed. Congress's spending is limited by the number of subjects they are authorized to address.

The enumerated powers is the budget.

We did not have a federal budget until Congress passed the Budget and Accounting Act of 1921. That act was unconstitutional since it required the president to submit a budget to Congress. The Constitution does not make any such requirement on the president, nor does it involve the president in the process of legislation in regard to spending appropriations beyond approving or vetoing the legislation. Accordingly, this legislation amends the Constitution by law rather than by amendment and Congress has no such authority.

Congress is to appropriate funds to carry out a handful of delegated powers, and then it pays the bills with receipts from taxes. The constitutional powers of the national government are to be exercised with the proceeds of excise taxes and imposed tariffs, with any shortfall made up by an apportioned assessment on the states based on population.

This is a complete list of the objects which Congress is lawfully authorized to spend money:

- The census, Article I, Section 2, clause 3.
- Publishing the journals of the House and Senate, Article I, Section 5, clause 3.
- Salaries of senators and representatives, Article I, Section 6, clause 1.
- Salaries of civil officers of the United States, Article I, Section 6, clause 2, and Article II, Section 1, clause 7.

- Pay the debts, Article I, Section 8, clause 1, and Article VI, clause 1.
- Pay tax collectors, Article I, Section 8, clause 1.
- Regulate commerce with foreign nations, among the several states, and with Indian tribes, Article I, Section 8, clause 3.
- Immigration office, Article I, Section 8, clause 4.
- The mint, Article I, Section 8, clause 5.
- Attorney General to handle the authorized federal litigation involving the national government, Article I, Section 8, clauses 6 and 10.
- Post offices and post roads, Article I, Section 8, clause 7.
- Patent and copyright office, Article I, Section 8, clause 8.
- Federal courts, Article I, Section 8, clause 9, and Article III, Section 1.
- Military and citizens' militia, Article I, Section 8, clause 11.
- Since Congress has general legislative authority over the federal enclaves listed in Article I, Section 8, next to last clause, Congress has broad spending authority over the areas listed in this clause.
- The President's entertainment expenses for foreign dignitaries, Article II, Section 3.
- Since Congress had general legislative authority over the Western Territory before it was broken up into states, Congress could appropriate funds for the U.S. Marshalls, federal judges, and similar expenses for those territories, Article IV, Section 3, clause 2.

Since Article VI defines the Constitution as the "supreme Law of the Land," spending outside the provided limits within the document is to be considered unlawful.

How about an amendment to call for a balanced budget?

All versions of a balanced budget amendment transform our federal Constitution from one which created a central government with only a few enumerated powers to a national government of general and unlimited powers. This is because balanced budget amendments typically substitute a budget for the enumerated powers. As a result, the national government would become lawfully authorized by the Constitution to spend money on whatever line item they put in the budget.

Since state governments were created to possess general and unlimited powers, state governments may lawfully spend tax money on just about anything they choose. The only prohibited subjects are those listed in Article I, section 10, of the national Constitution and those prohibited by their own state constitutions.

Since the states possess general and unlimited powers, they need budgets to limit spending to receipts.

Related Questions and Research Assignments

1. Reading assignment: Read Article II.

2. Paraphrase the following segment of James Madison's Federalist Paper No. 45:

   "The powers delegated by the proposed Constitution to the federal government are few and defined. Those which are to remain in the State governments are numerous and indefinite. The former will be exercised principally on external objects, as war, peace, negotiation, and foreign commerce; with which last the power of taxation will, for the most part, be connected. The powers reserved to the several States will extend to all the objects which, in the ordinary course of affairs, concern the lives, liberties, and properties of the people, and the internal order, improvement, and prosperity of the State."

3. Paraphrase the following segment of Alexander Hamilton's Federalist Paper No. 16:

   "But if the execution of the laws of the national government should not require the intervention of the State legislatures, if they were to pass into immediate operation upon the citizens themselves, the particular governments could not interrupt their progress without an open and violent exertion of an unconstitutional power. No omissions nor evasions would answer the end. They would be obliged to act, and in such a manner as would leave no doubt that they had encroached on the national rights. An experiment of this nature would always be hazardous in the face of a constitution in any degree competent to its own defense, and of a people enlightened enough to distinguish between a legal exercise and an illegal usurpation of authority. The success of it would require not merely a factious majority in the legislature, but the concurrence of the courts of justice and of the body of the people. If the judges were not embarked in a conspiracy with the legislature, they would pronounce the resolutions of such a majority to be contrary to the supreme law of the land, unconstitutional, and void. If the people were not tainted with the spirit of their State representatives, they, as the natural guardians of the Constitution, would throw their weight into the national scale and give it a decided preponderancy in the contest. Attempts of this kind would not often be made with levity or rashness, because they could seldom be made without danger to the authors, unless in cases of a tyrannical exercise of the federal authority."

4. Research assignment: List five of the federal Executive Departments, and the federal Executive agencies under each one. Based on your understanding of this chapter, of the department and/or agencies that you listed, which departments and/or agencies are unconstitutional and therefore should not exist? State your reasons why.

5. Research assignment: Find three federal criminal laws, that are unconstitutional. Remember to prove why they are unconstitutional by using only original sources.

6. In the "General Welfare Clause" section above, pick one of the segments shown for Federalist No. 41 and explain how it helps you understand the founders' intent of the general welfare clause.

7. Use a highlighter of your choice, go to the back of the book in the reference section and look at the Constitution. Go through the Articles, including amendments, and highlight the powers given to Congress in one color. Next, use a highlighter of a different color, go back through the Articles and highlight the powers of the president. Next, use a different color to highlight the powers of the courts. Use a fourth color and go to Article I, Section 10, to highlight the

few powers the states agreed to give up in order to form a limited central government.

8. From reading this chapter, how should federal criminal laws differ from State criminal laws?

9. In the "Commerce Clause" section in the above chapter, you were referred to four of The Federalist Papers, numbered 22, 42, 44, and 56. Which one, in your opinion, has the most substance to it and why? Describe what the author is saying in the one you have selected.

10. Which of The Federalist Papers listed in the above question would you say are more general in nature?

Chapter 4

ENUMERATED POWERS OF THE PRESIDENT

On election night, November 2, 2010, the Speaker of the House of Representatives, John Boehner said in his victory speech, "While our new majority will serve as your voice in the people's House, we must remember it is the president who sets the agenda for our government."

Where in the Constitution does it say the president sets the agenda for the government?

It is our Constitution which sets the agenda for the federal government, not the president.

The powers of the president are limited and defined by our Constitution in Article II, just like it does for Congress in Article I. In Federalist Paper No. 71, last paragraph, Alexander Hamilton asks:

> "...if they have been able, on a recent occasion, to make the monarch tremble at the prospect of an innovation attempted by them, what would be to be feared from an elective magistrate of four years' duration, with the confined authorities of a President of the United States?"

The answer to Hamilton's question is this: There would be nothing to fear if presidents obeyed the confined authorities listed in the Constitution.

Hamilton explained those confined authorities in Federalist Paper No. 75, third paragraph:

"The essence of the legislative authority is to enact laws, or, in other words, to prescribe rules for the regulation of the society; while the execution of the laws, and the employment of the common strength, either for this purpose or for the common defense, seem to comprise all the functions of the executive magistrate."

Consider the president's powers below. They are confined and limited to carrying out laws made by Congress and to enforcing certain judicial opinions, military defense, appointing officials subject to Congress's approval, and entertaining foreign dignitaries.

This is the complete list of the president's enumerated powers:

1. Article I, Section 7, clauses 2 and 3, grants to the president the power to approve or veto bills and resolutions passed by Congress. If Congress does not pass any bills, then the president has nothing to do here.

2. Article I, Section 9, next to last clause, grants to the Treasury Department of the Executive Branch the power to write checks pursuant to authorized appropriations made by Congress. If Congress does not appropriate any money, then the president has nothing to do here. If they appropriate money for matters they are not authorized to address, he may refuse to write the checks.

3. Article II, Section 1, clause1, vests executive power, explained below, in the president.

4. Article II, Section 1, last clause, sets forth the presidential oath of office to "preserve, protect and defend the Constitution of the United States."

5. Article II, Section 2, clause 1, gives the president the authority to:

   • Act as Commander in Chief of the armed forces once they have been called by Congress into the actual service of the United States, and then only for the three reasons authorized. Notice that he is not the Commander in Chief unless Congress "calls" the militia into service. How does Congress call for actual service? The only way provided in the Constitution is by a declaration of war pursuant to Article I, Section 8, clause 11, as they did in World War I and II. This was not done in the Korean War, the Vietnam War, nor for any of the worldwide conflicts in which we have been involved since then. Note also that Congress has the power to determine the funding for the military in the twelfth clause, so the conflicts could be stopped at anytime. If Congress does not declare a war nor fund it, the president has nothing to do here either.

- Require the principal officers in the Executive branch to provide written opinions upon the duties of their offices.
- Grant reprieves and pardons for offenses against the United States, but he cannot stop impeachments of any federal judge or federal officer.

6. Article II, Section 2, clause 2, grants the president the power:

- To make treaties, but only with the advice and consent of the senate. If the senate does not want a treaty, the president has nothing to do here.
- To nominate ambassadors, other public ministers and consuls, federal judges, and various other officers, but only with the advice and consent of the senate.

7. Article II, Section 2, clause 3, grants the president the power to make recess appointments, which expire at the end of Congress's next session.

8. Article II, Section 3:

- Imposes the duty on the president to periodically advise Congress on the state of the Union, and authorizes the president to recommend to Congress such measures as he deems wise. He does not have the authority to act, or to dictate, only to recommend.

- Authorizes the president, on extraordinary occasions, to convene one or both houses of Congress, such as when he asks Congress to declare war. If the House of Representatives and Senate cannot agree on when to adjourn, he is then authorized to adjourn them to such time as he deems proper.
- Imposes the duty upon the president to receive ambassadors and other public ministers.
- Imposes the duty upon the president to take care that the laws are faithfully executed. Imposes the duty upon the president to commission all of the officers of the United States.

Anything the president does beyond this list of duties is considered unconstitutional and a usurpation of powers which were not granted.

What is executive power?

The executive power is the power to put into effect those acts of Congress which are within Congress's enumerated powers. It is not a blank check giving him power to do whatever he wants.

If Congress establishes a "uniform Rule of Naturalization" as authorized by Article I, Section 8, clause 4, it is the president's duty to implement and enforce the law which Congress makes. The president is to execute only the authorized acts of Congress.

His oath of office shows that the president must use his independent judgment as to which acts of Congress are and are not constitutional. The president has the duty, imposed by his oath, to act as a check on Congress and refuse to enforce unconstitutional laws and/or federal court opinions. The president's duty is not to go along with Congress nor is it to obey the courts. The president must make his own independent determinations. He may not abdicate this duty in favor of another branch. The Executive Branch is to function as a check on the other two branches.

Otherwise, he would be in collusion with the legislative branch to usurp power over the people. Madison says in Federalist Paper No. 44, last paragraph:

> "...the success of the usurpation will depend on the executive and judiciary departments, which are to expound and give effect to the legislative acts..."

Acting as a check on Congress and federal courts by refusing to enforce unconstitutional laws and court opinions, as well as the duty of entertaining foreign dignitaries, are the only occasions when the president may act alone.

Administrative Law

Article I, Section 1, of the U.S. Constitution says:

> "All legislative Powers herein granted shall be vested in a Congress of the United States, which shall consist of a Senate and House of Representatives."

That little phrase is of immense importance. It means Congress alone may make laws. Laws are to be made only by representatives who we can fire every two years, and by senators who we can fire every six years. There is no permission for Congress to delegate that authority to another branch. The job is theirs and theirs alone.

Merriam-Webster's first definition of a law is: "a binding custom or practice of a community: a rule of conduct or action prescribed or formally recognized as binding or enforced by a controlling authority."

Administrative law is the creation of rules by executive agencies.

Most of the existing federal executive agencies are unconstitutional because they were created to address subjects the federal government has no constitutional authority to address.

Below is a partial list of the unconstitutional federal executive departments/agencies that make laws and rules in today's government:

- Department of Agriculture.
- Department of Labor.
- Department of Health and Human Services.
- Department of Housing and Urban Development.
- Department of Energy.
- Department of Education.
- Department of Transportation.
- Department of Homeland Security.

- Environmental Protection Agency.
- Federal Communications Commission.
- Office of Science and Technology Policy.
- Office of National Drug Control Policy.
- National Economic Council.
- Small Business Administration.
- Council on Environmental Quality.
- Bureau of Land Management.

There are fifteen listed federal executive departments and over 130 related administrative agencies, most of which are unconstitutional.

To complicate matters, some of these executive departments and agencies have their own enforcement arms, like the Bureau of Alcohol, Tobacco, and Firearms which is under the executive Department of Justice. Another example is the Transportation Safety Agency, commonly referred to as the TSA.

A study of history shows that during the administration of Woodrow Wilson, Congress delegated its law-making powers to agencies within the Executive Branch. Since then, Congress has passed legislation such as the Clean Air Act of 1970 designed to reduce nationwide air pollution. The Act created and delegated the details to be written by unelected, unaccountable bureaucrats in the various executive agencies, such as the EPA (Environmental Protection Agency), or OSHA (Occupational Safety and Health Administration). Those executive agencies write the administrative rules which implement the legislation. The result is the complex code of federal regulations which is accepted by lawyers as law.

Here is just one example out of thousands of such unconstitutional legislation by Congress, resulting in unlawful lawmaking by those in the executive department.

The below is from the EPA's own website.

"The EPA regulates the use of pesticides under the authority of two federal statutes: the Federal Insecticide,

Fungicide, and Rodenticide Act (FIFRA) and the Federal Food, Drug, and Cosmetic Act (FFDCA)."

A subsequent paragraph explains:

"The Federal Insecticide, Fungicide, and Rodenticide Act (FIFRA) provides the basis for regulation, sale, distribution and use of pesticides in the U.S. FIFRA authorizes EPA to review and register pesticides for specified uses. EPA also has the authority to suspend or cancel the registration of a pesticide if subsequent information shows that continued use would pose unreasonable risks. According to the law passed by Congress, the EPA may make laws regarding product licensing. Any company who manufacturers, transports, or sells pesticides must register with this Executive agency. Registration is based on a risk versus benefit standard. The FIFRA legislation has strong authority to require manufacturers to provide information on the detrimental effects of the particular products to the EPA. In addition, the EPA would have the authority to regulate pesticides through labeling, packaging, composition, and disposal. The EPA would also have the authority to grant exemptions, to suspend or cancel a product's registration, control the appeals process, etc."

The EPA says above that if you manufacture, transport, sell, label, package, assemble, or dispose of a pesticide, then they may regulate your activities. This is just one of the infinite subjects the Constitution left to the states or to the people to decide, not the federal government. Consider the number of regulations a manufacturer of pesticides, along with the related industries, must contend with just to stay on the legal side of the federal government.

Executive Orders

May the president lawfully make executive orders?

The guiding principle is this: The president has no authority to do anything apart from constitutional authority or statutory authority, assuming the statute itself is constitutional.

Respecting those matters within his constitutional authority and duties, the president may make orders. The term "executive orders" has been coined to describe them.

For example, Article II, Section 3, says it is the president's constitutional duty "to take care that the Laws be faithfully executed." He has the duty to enforce constitutional laws made by Congress. How does he enforce the laws? Sometimes, by means of orders.

Assume Congress originates a law, as authorized by Article I, Section 8, clause 6, making it a felony to counterfeit the securities and current coin of the United States. If U.S. attorneys are not prosecuting counterfeiters, the president should order them to do it or fire them.

Assume Congress creates a law which purports to make possession of shotguns shorter than 18 inches a crime. Since the presidential oath requires him to "preserve, protect and defend the Constitution," he is obligated to order the U.S. Attorney General and the U.S. attorneys to refuse to prosecute anyone for possession of sawed-off shotguns. Why? Such a law is unconstitutional because it is outside the scope of the legislative powers granted to Congress in our Constitution. It also violates the intent of the second amendment.

When Congress passes an unconstitutional law, the president must refuse to implement it. He may, by means of executive orders, instruct people in the Executive Branch not to comply. If a president orders the U.S. attorneys not to prosecute persons for possession of sawed-off shotguns, he is acting lawfully because Congress has no authority to ban them.

Such an order to refuse prosecution falls within the president's constitutional duties to enforce the Constitution, and he is giving an order to people within the Executive Branch. The president is the one who is responsible for carrying out the acts of Congress since he has the executive power, but, because of his oath, he may not carry out unconstitutional laws. That is one of the checks on Congress.

The president may also make orders which address housekeeping issues within the Executive Branch, such as dress codes or smoking and drinking on the job. He may also encourage executive agencies to hire qualified handicapped people for instance.

Presidents down through the ages have issued various executive orders which are unlawful because they are not authorized by the Constitution or by constitutional acts of Congress. Here are two current executive orders which are particularly pernicious because they undermine our foundational principle of federalism which was discussed earlier by the improper consolidation of the states into one republic:

1. E.O.13575–Establishment of the White House Rural Council. This executive order provides for over 25 federal departments and agencies to run aspects respecting rural life.

2. E.O. 13528–Establishing Council of Governors. The effect of this executive order is to erase the independence and sovereignty of the states and to consolidate them into a national system under the authority of the Executive Branch.

These executive orders are unconstitutional as usurpations of powers which are not granted within the Constitution. States have the constitutional authority to simply nullify the orders since there is no agreement in the Constitution by the states not to do so.

Our framers warned against the consolidation of the sovereign states into one national sovereignty. In Federalist Paper No. 32, 2nd paragraph, Hamilton writes:

> "An entire consolidation of the States into one complete national sovereignty would imply an entire subordination of the parts; and whatever powers might remain in them, would be altogether dependent on the general will. But as the plan of the convention aims only at a partial union or consolidation, the State governments would clearly retain all the rights of sovereignty which they before had, and which were not, by that act, EXCLUSIVELY delegated to the United States."

Federalist Paper No. 62, 6th paragraph, says:

> "In this spirit it may be remarked, that the equal vote allowed to each State is at once a constitutional recognition of the portion of sovereignty remaining in the individual States, and an instrument for preserving that residuary sovereignty. So far the equality ought to be no less acceptable to the large than to the small States; since they are not less solicitous to guard, by every possible expedient, against an improper consolidation of the States into one simple republic."

And in Federalist Paper No. 39, 7th paragraph, Madison says:

> "'But it was not sufficient,' say the adversaries of the proposed Constitution, 'for the convention to adhere to the republican form. They ought, with equal care, to have preserved the FEDERAL form, which regards the Union as a CONFEDERACY of sovereign states; instead of which, they have framed a NATIONAL government, which regards the Union as a CONSOLIDATION of the States.' And it is asked by what authority this bold and radical innovation was undertaken? The handle which has been

made of this objection requires that it should be examined with some precision."

Madison then gives an exposition of the national and federal aspects of our Constitution. More than any other, Federalist Paper No. 39 addresses the founders' primary distinction between a national and a federal government. The founders held the belief that the states enjoyed an elevated status over the central government.

In summation, the president must always uphold our Constitution.

His main job is to carry out constitutional acts of Congress.

The president violates the Constitution when he implements rules and laws made by unconstitutional departments and agencies in his Executive Branch because the president and executive agencies, as well as Congress, do not have authority over these subjects.

What is the remedy for these violations of the Constitution?

In Federalist Paper No. 66, Hamilton states that impeachment is an essential check on a president who encroaches on the powers of Congress. Federalist Paper No. 77 points out that impeachment is the remedy for "abuse of the executive authority."

But failing that, if Congress does not honor their oath to protect the Constitution, the states, counties, cities, and citizens must nullify unconstitutional executive orders and administrative rules. The only other choice outside active rebellion is to obey and submit to the destruction of our constitutional republic as it was designed.

Since state and county officials, in Article VI, last clause, have also taken the oath to support the U.S. Constitution, they are bound by oath to refuse to submit to illegal executive orders and illegal agency rules.

Impeachment

There is a widespread misconception that it is almost necessary for the president, federal judges, and staff members to commit a felony before they may be impeached and removed.

That is not true. Alexander Hamilton points out that the president may be impeached and removed for mere usurpations.

For the executive department, Federalist Paper No. 66, 2nd paragraph, Hamilton says:

> "An absolute or qualified negative in the executive upon the acts of the legislative body, is admitted, by the ablest adepts in political science, to be an indispensable barrier against the encroachments of the latter upon the former. And it may, perhaps, with no less reason be contended, that the powers relating to impeachments are, as before intimated, an essential check in the hands of that body upon the encroachments of the executive."

For the federal judges, Hamilton points out in Federalist Paper No. 81, 8th paragraph, that federal judges may be impeached and removed for usurpations:

> "Particular misconstructions and contraventions of the will of the legislature may now and then happen; but they can never be so extensive as to amount to an inconvenience, or in any sensible degree to affect the order of the political system. This may be inferred with certainty, from the general nature of the judicial power, from the objects to which it relates, from the manner in which it is exercised, from its comparative weakness, and from its total incapacity to support its usurpations by force. And the inference is greatly fortified by the

consideration of the important constitutional check which the power of instituting impeachments in one part of the legislative body, and of determining upon them in the other, would give to that body upon the members of the judicial department. This is alone a complete security. There never can be danger that the judges, by a series of deliberate usurpations on the authority of the legislature, would hazard the united resentment of the body intrusted with it, while this body was possessed of the means of punishing their presumption, by degrading them from their stations."

Throughout The Federalist Papers, it is stated that impeachment is for political offenses.

The House of Representatives has the sole power of impeachment, Article I, Section 2, last clause.

The senate has the sole power to try all impeachments, Article I, Section 3, next to last clause.

The opinion to convict is not able to be reviewed by any other body. Thus the House of Representatives may impeach, and the senate may convict for any reason whatsoever, no matter how small, and their decision cannot be overturned.

The language of Article II, Section 4 about "Treason, Bribery, or other high Crimes and Misdemeanors" could use more explanation to get to the founder's intent. Again, we will refer to Webster's 1828 dictionary.

Misdemeanor had a much broader meaning than simply a lesser category of criminal offenses as it does today when speaking about political offenses rather than legal offenses. Legal offenses are a different matter.

Webster's 1828 Dictionary shows the primary meaning of misdemeanor to be:

"Ill behavior; evil conduct; fault; mismanagement."

This proves that the president, vice-president, and all civil officers of the United States may be impeached, tried, convicted, and removed from office for something as simple as mismanagement.

As illustrated above, the founders intended for those in the executive department, including the president and federal judges to walk a fine line just to stay in office. Should their actions exceed the specific bounds that were given as you learned above, they would be subject to impeachment by the Legislative Branch.

Treaties

What are the limits of making treaties? Can we make treaties on any subject the president deems proper and which Congress ratifies?

If the United States Senate ratifies the United Nations Convention on the Rights of the Child, will that UN Convention become part of the supreme law of the land as an authorized treaty?

If the senate ratifies the proposed cap and trade climate treaty, will that become part of the supreme law of the land?

Is it true that whenever the senate ratifies a treaty, it becomes part of the supreme law of the land?

Not necessarily. The question that we must always ask is, "Where exactly is this authorized in the Constitution?"

As mentioned in earlier sections, the constitution grants the executive branch the authority to make treaties. However, according to Article II, Section 2, clause 2, the senate must also approve.

Additionally, Article VI, clause 2 says:

> "This Constitution, and the Laws of the United States which shall be made in Pursuance thereof; and all Treaties made, or which shall be made, under the Authority of the United States, shall be the supreme Law of the Land; and the Judges in every State shall be bound thereby, any Thing in the Constitution or Laws of any State to the Contrary notwithstanding."

From this we see that the federal government is authorized to make treaties, but what are the limitations, if any, are on this treaty-making power? Can treaties be about any subject? Or, are the proper objects of treaties limited by the Constitution?

In a classic rule of construction, one must give effect to every word and phrase. The Constitution does not say, "Treaties made by the United States are part of the supreme law of the land."

Instead, it says that treaties made "under the authority of the United States", are part of the supreme law of the land. So a treaty is part of the supreme law of the land only if it is made under the authority of the United States.

The Constitution is the "authority" of the United States. The Constitution limits the subjects they may address by virtue of having only enumerated powers.

The president and senate must be authorized in the Constitution to act on a subject before any treaty made by them on that subject qualifies as part of the supreme law of the land.

If the Constitution does not authorize the president and congress to act on an object, the treaty is not law. It is a mere usurpation, and deserves to be treated as such.

Because the Constitution is considered fundamental law, according to Federalist Paper No. 78 the Constitution is the standard by which the legitimacy of all presidential acts, all acts of Congress, all treaties, and all judicial opinions are measured.

In Federalist Paper No. 44, last paragraph, James Madison said a treaty which violates a state constitution would have no effect in that state:

> "In the third place, as the constitutions of the States differ much from each other, it might happen that a treaty or national law, of great and equal importance to the States, would interfere with some and not with other constitutions, and would consequently be valid in some of the States, at the same time that it would have no effect in others."

Jefferson wrote extensively on treaties, and the powers granted by the constitution. Even though this information is not included in The Federalist Papers, these writings provide an insight into the intentions of the founders. For example, in Thomas Jefferson's Anas, 1793, he wrote:

> "In giving to the President and Senate a power to make treaties, the Constitution meant only to authorize them to carry into effect, by way of treaty, any powers they might constitutionally exercise."

In the Parliamentary Manual, 1800, Jefferson wrote:

> "Surely the President and Senate cannot do by treaty what the whole government is interdicted from doing in any way."

And in a letter from Jefferson to James Madison in 1796, he wrote:

> "According to the rule established by usage and common sense, of construing one part of the instrument by another, the objects on which the President and Senate may exclusively act by treaty are much reduced, but the field on which they may act with the sanction of the Legislature is large enough; and I see no harm in rendering their sanction necessary, and not much harm in annihilating the whole treaty-making power, except as to making peace."

We have seen that the treaty-making power of the United States is limited. What, then, are the proper objects of treaties?

To find the answer, we must go to the Constitution to see what it authorizes the president and congress to do in this area.

The Constitution delegates to congress powers to:

- "To regulate Commerce with foreign Nations...and with the Indian Tribes," Article I, Section 8, clause 3.

- "To declare War...and make Rules concerning Captures on Land and Water," Article I, Section 8, clause 11.

The Constitution authorizes the president to "appoint Ambassadors, other public Ministers and Consuls," Article II, Section 2, clause 2.

The authors of The Federalist Papers commented on the treaty- making power of the United States. John Jay said, in Federalist Paper No. 64, that treaties relate to war, peace, commerce, and to the promotion of trade and navigation.

Madison said treaties also relate to sending and receiving ambassadors and consuls and to commerce in Federalist Paper No. 42. There may be additional objects of the treaty-making power authorized in the Constitution. For example, Article I, Section 8, clause 8, authorizes Congress "To promote the Progress of Science and useful Arts, by securing for limited Times to Authors and Inventors the exclusive Right to their respective Writings and Discoveries." The United States is able to enter into treaties respecting patents and copyrights.

With that background, what if there was a proposed treaty titled "United Nations Convention on the Rights of the Child" and assume it had been ratified by the senate, would it become part of "the supreme law of the land?"

To answer that question, we must first ask: Does the Constitution grant to either congress or the president the power to make laws respecting the subject of children? The answer is no.

Thus jurisdiction over children is reserved to the states or the people which is also affirmed in the 10th Amendment.

Accordingly, if the senate were to ratify the United Nations Convention on the Rights of the Child, the treaty would not become part of the supreme law of this land because it would not have been made under the authority of the United States. It would be a mere usurpation and would deserve to be treated as such.

If the senate were to ratify the Cap and Trade climate treaty, which, among other things, would force energy companies to buy allowances or permits for their carbon emissions, would it become part of the supreme law of the land?

The federal government may not lawfully circumvent the U.S. Constitution by international treaties. It may not act by treaty what it is not permitted to do by the U.S. Constitution.

In a letter to James Monroe in 1796, Thomas Jefferson pointed to a legislative remedy if the president and the senate ignore the constitutional limits on the treaty-making power of the United States. Thomas Jefferson said:

> "We conceive the constitutional doctrine to be, that though the President and Senate have the general power of making treaties, yet wherever they include in a treaty matters confided by the Constitution to the three branches of Legislature, an *act of legislation* will be requisite to confirm these articles, and that the House of Representatives, as one branch of the Legislature, are perfectly free to pass the act or to refuse it, governing themselves by their own judgment whether it is for the good of their constituents to let the treaty go into effect or not."

Jefferson is saying that if a treaty is ratified, and if it is committed to the care of the house, the senate, and the president, then legislation would be required to add strength to the treaty. In those situations, the House of Representatives would be involved as well. Two years later, he goes on to confirm that point in a letter to James Madison in 1798:

> "I was glad...to hear it admitted on all hands, that laws of the United States, subsequent to a treaty, control its operation, and that the Legislature is the only power which can control a treaty. Both points are sound beyond doubt."

No other nation has such a unique governmental system of checks on their central government as our founders gave us in the Constitution.

Related Questions and Research Assignments

1. Read Article III

2. Paraphrase the following segment of James Madison's Federalist Paper No. 44:

> "If it be asked what is to be the consequence, in case the Congress shall misconstrue this part of the Constitution, and exercise powers not warranted by its true meaning, I answer, the same as if they should misconstrue or enlarge any other power vested in them; as if the general power had been reduced to particulars, and any one of these were to be violated; the same, in short, as if the State legislatures should violate the irrespective constitutional authorities. In the first instance, the success of the usurpation will depend on the executive and judiciary departments, which are to expound and give effect to the legislative acts; and in the last resort a remedy must be obtained from the people who can, by the election of more faithful representatives, annul the acts of the usurpers. The truth is, that this ultimate redress may be more confided in against unconstitutional acts of the federal than of the State legislatures, for this plain reason, that as every such act of the former will be an invasion of the rights of the latter, these will be ever ready to mark the innovation, to sound the alarm to the people, and to exert their local influence in effecting a change of federal representatives. There being no such intermediate body between the State legislatures and the people interested in watching the conduct of the former, violations of the State constitutions are more likely to remain unnoticed and unredressed."

3. Paraphrase the following segment of Alexander Hamilton's Federalist Paper No. 78. This goes back to Hamilton's affirmation,

and the states' agreement, that Congress does not have the authority to make laws outside the strict confines of the enumerated powers. Are they really laws, or not law at all?

"Some perplexity respecting the rights of the courts to pronounce legislative acts void, because contrary to the Constitution, has arisen from an imagination that the doctrine would imply a superiority of the judiciary to the legislative power. It is urged that the authority which can declare the acts of another void, must necessarily be superior to the one whose acts may be declared void. As this doctrine is of great importance in all the American constitutions, a brief discussion of the ground on which it rests cannot be unacceptable.

There is no position which depends on clearer principles, than that every act of a delegated authority, contrary to the tenor of the commission under which it is exercised, is void. No legislative act, therefore, contrary to the Constitution, can be valid. To deny this, would be to affirm, that the deputy is greater than his principal; that the servant is above his master; that the representatives of the people are superior to the people themselves; that men acting by virtue of powers, may do not only what their powers do not authorize, but what they forbid."

4. Research NAFTA (North American Free Trade Agreement) and give the reasons it is or is not a lawful, constitutional treaty.

5. Look up the definition of a "democracy" and compare/contrast it to the definition of a "republic." Use the Webster's Dictionary of 1828 only. The Internet address is: http://webstersdictionary1828.com

6. Compare and/or contrast a government under socialism to a republic. What role does the president play in each?

7. What part does the president play in any impeachment process? Prove your answer using original sources only.

8. If the president chooses not to wear a tie to a formal governmental event, could Congress impeach and remove him/her from office if they did not like that gesture?

9. If the president negotiates a treaty that is then ratified by the senate but is contradictory to the Constitution, is it still valid? Why or why not? What do you think would be the proper remedy in such a case?

Chapter 5

ENUMERATED POWERS OF THE FEDERAL COURTS

Article III establishes our justice system with one Supreme Court and gives Congress the power to establish, or not, lower federal courts.

Judicial power refers to a court's power to hear and issue opinions on certain cases.

This chapter addresses the limited role given by the people to the federal courts and how the judges have used two ways to violate the Constitution:

- By accepting cases and issuing opinions on subjects they have no authority to address.
- Redefining certain natural rights as constitutional rights so that they can rule on them. Once a right is determined to "arise under the Constitution," the federal courts have assumed the power to make rulings on the subject.

Several case opinions are included to illustrate why they are or are not considered the law of the land.

Article I, Section 8, clause 9, authorizes Congress to create courts inferior to the Supreme Court. As a result, Congress has set up 94 federal district courts and thirteen circuit courts of appeal, eleven numbered circuits plus the DC Circuit Court and the Federal Circuit Court.

The trials of most federal cases take place in the district courts. The loser may appeal to the circuit court of appeal for that district. The Supreme Court hears some appeals from the circuit courts of appeal.

Article III, Section 2, limits the cases which federal courts are permitted to hear.

Federal courts may hear cases which:

- Arise under the Constitution, or the laws of the United States, or treaties made under the authority of the United States.
- Affect ambassadors, other public ministers and consuls; cases of admiralty and maritime jurisdiction; or cases in which the United States is a party.
- Between two or more states.
- Between citizens of different states.
- Between citizens of the same state who claim lands under grants of different states.

These are the only cases which federal courts have constitutional authority to hear.

There were two more cases they were originally allowed to hear, but those cases were revoked by the 11th Amendment.

Alexander Hamilton wrote in Federalist Paper No. 83, 8th paragraph:

> "In like manner the judicial authority of the federal judicatures is declared by the Constitution to comprehend certain cases particularly specified. The expression of those cases marks the precise limits, beyond which the federal courts cannot extend their jurisdiction, because the objects of their cognizance being enumerated, the specification would be nugatory if it did not exclude all ideas of more extensive authority."

Just as the enumerated powers of Congress is the foundation for understanding the original intent of the Constitution, so is the need to understand the limited and fine line which the founders intended the federal judges to walk in order to keep from being impeached and sent home.

Article III, Section 1, explains:

> "The judicial Power of the United States, shall be vested in one supreme Court, and in such inferior Courts as the Congress may from time to time ordain and establish. The Judges, both of the supreme and inferior Courts, shall hold their Offices during good Behaviour, and shall, at Stated Times, receive for their Services a Compensation which shall not be diminished during their Continuance in Office."

Notice they are to keep their jobs only if they display good behavior.

Does good behavior include the acceptance of cases which they are not authorized to decide?

Does good behavior include offering opinions which are contrary to the intent of the Constitution?

Who decides?

Congress decides by the authoritative use of their power of impeachment and adherence to their oath to "support" the Constitution. The President may also decide by refusing to enforce unconstitutional opinions in adhering to his oath to "defend" the Constitution.

Article VI of the Constitution does not say that Supreme Court opinions are automatically considered the "Supreme Law of the Land." For that to happen, the laws and opinions offered must be made in pursuance of the Constitution. They must pertain to the few enumerated powers listed in the Constitution.

Are state laws criminalizing job discrimination or state laws criminalizing abortion or state laws criminalizing homosexual conduct objects of the judicial power of the federal courts? No.

Do these subjects "arise" under the Constitution? No.

Do any of these laws fit any subjects the federal government may address for the nations as a whole? No.

Do any of these laws relate to treaties made under the authority of the United States? No.

Several states have passed laws which require voters to have documented identification in order to vote. However, several lower federal courts have gotten involved in those cases and issued opinions that were contrary to the states' laws.

Is voter qualification an object of the judicial power of the federal courts? No.

Do these state laws fit within any of the categories of cases which federal courts are authorized to hear? No.

In Federalist Paper No. 80, Hamilton commented on each of the itemized proper objects of judicial authority. But we will consider only cases "arising under the Constitution," which concern the execution of the provisions in the Constitution.

One example Hamilton described was if a state decided to enter into a treaty with France, then that state violates Article I, Section 10, because the states are prohibited from entering into treaties. In that case, the federal courts are in the best position to overrule infractions which are "in manifest contravention of the articles of Union."

In other words, if the states decide not to honor the limits they agreed to Article I, Section 10, then the federal courts will have jurisdiction to take any cases filed against them.

But the federal courts have evaded the constitutional limits on their power to hear cases by fabricating individual constitutional rights. If the topic under consideration is a constitutional right, then the courts can say that those particular cases "arise under the Constitution."

Recall that earlier in this text, the distinction was made between natural rights and constitutional rights. In Roe v. Wade (1973), seven judges on the U.S. Supreme Court said a *constitutional* right of privacy, founded in the 14th Amendment's concept of personal liberty, gave them, not the states, the authority to rule on abortion as a federal criminal offense.

These seven judges just redefined a natural right as a constitutional right by labeling "privacy" to be a constitutional right.

Accordingly, using the 14th Amendment, they said that states are prohibited from outlawing abortion on the basis that personal privacy is a constitutional right.

In Lawrence v. Texas (2003), six judges on the U.S. Supreme Court said in their opinion, cited below, that a Texas law which criminalized homosexual conduct was unconstitutional because it violated practitioners' "...right to liberty under the Due Process Clause" (p.578), "...of the Fourteenth Amendment" (pp. 564, 579).

Nothing in our Constitution prohibits the states from making laws that declare abortion or homosexual conduct to be crimes and nothing in our Constitution grants rights to individuals to engage in these practices.

Federal judges have used the 14th Amendment as a blank check to prevent the states from outlawing conduct which they have chosen to legalize. They made up a constitutional right to do those things. What if they had decided that the 14th Amendment did not intend the states to forbid segregated schools, when, in fact, they have no jurisdiction over the subjects of segregation or integration for the nation as a whole?

Under this view, their powers are not limited.

If a state makes it a crime to rape a child, five judges on the Supreme Court can fabricate a constitutional "liberty" or "privacy" right to have sex with children by using the 14th Amendment, disregarding the state law.

THE HANDBOOK FOR WE THE PEOPLE

Can they mandate, under federal penalty, that all couples must produce at least four children or have a doctor's excuse why they cannot? Can they mandate that all citizens must go to church, no matter what your state law says? What's the limit? Their view does not have any limits.

Adherence to strict construction of the Constitution by all three branches of our federal government is essential in order to ensure that every citizen's natural rights are protected regardless of their political persuasion.

Anthony Kennedy, Supreme Court judge, who wrote the majority opinion in Lawrence v. Texas, said on page 579 of the opinion:

> "As the Constitution endures, persons in every generation
> can invoke its principles in their own search for greater
> freedom."

Judge Kennedy's opinion above does not recognize the limits of Article III, Section 2.

The U.S. Congress is not authorized to make laws, for or against, such subjects as abortion, homosexual conduct, religion, family size, drugs, contraception, etc. for the nation as a whole. Again, these are subjects reserved to the states, or the people.

100 | BOB HILLIARD

Due Process Clause

What does the due process clause of the 14th Amendment really mean?

It says: "...nor shall any State deprive any person of life, liberty, or property, without due process of law..."

Raoul Berger (1901–2000) was an attorney and professor at the University of California at Berkeley and Harvard University School of Law. While at Harvard, he was the Charles Warren Senior Fellow in American Legal History. As a result of his extensive historic research on the founder's intent with the 14th Amendment, he set out his findings in a book, *Government by Judiciary: The Transformation of the Fourteenth Amendment.*

The clause, due process of law, is a well-known term with a narrow meaning going back to the Magna Charta.

At the time, the purpose of the due process clause of the 14th Amendment was to protect freed slaves from death, imprisonment, or having their possessions taken away except pursuant to the judgment of their peers after a fair trial where they could appear, cross-examine witnesses, and put on a defense.

Professor Berger points out that due process of law refers only to trials, to judicial proceedings in courts of justice. But, as shown above, some federal judges have used it to redefine terms like life, liberty, or property to be something other than a natural right so they can override state laws.

When federal judges redefine terms in the Constitution, they amend the Constitution in violation of Article V. They have no such authority.

Article V sets forth the two lawful methods of amending the Constitution. Redefinition by judges is not one of the lawful methods.

Most law schools teach that the Supreme Court is the ultimate authority on the Constitution, and when they, or a majority of five, speak, all must accept and obey. But that is not correct.

Are there remedies for this judicial lawlessness? Yes.

1. Congress must impeach and remove federal judges who usurp power. Judges do not have lifetime appointments, contrary to popular opinion, as they can be impeached, convicted, and removed from the bench for usurping power.

   They serve during "good Behaviour" only according to Article III, Section 1 of the Constitution. Hamilton discusses impeachment by Congress of usurping judges in Federalist Paper No. 81, 8th paragraph.

2. The president must refuse to go along with unconstitutional opinions. The president is bound by oath to reject unconstitutional laws even when approved by the Supreme Court. Hamilton understood that it might be appropriate for a president to refuse to enforce a federal court opinion. He says in Federalist Paper No. 78, 7th paragraph:

   > "The Executive not only dispenses the honors, but holds the sword of the community. The legislature not only commands the purse, but prescribes the rules by which the duties and rights of every citizen are to be regulated. The judiciary, on the contrary, has no influence over either the sword or the purse; no direction either of the strength or of the wealth of the society; and can take no active resolution whatever. It may truly be said to have neither FORCE nor WILL, but merely judgment; and must ultimately depend upon the aid of the executive arm even for the efficacy of its judgments."

3. The states have the natural right of self defense and must nullify unconstitutional opinions. State officers and judges

are bound by oath to support the Constitution in Article VI, last clause. So they, too, are honor bound to refuse to comply with unconstitutional federal court opinions, as well as unconstitutional federal laws, executive orders, and treaties which affect them and their citizens.

4. Our framers knew that we the people must be involved. Our framers understood that judges could be dangerous, but could not get away with it unless we concurred with them.

Hamilton says in Federalist Paper No.16 that "an illegal usurpation of authority," to be successful, "would require not merely a factious majority in the legislature, but the concurrence of the courts of justice and of the body of the people."

Because judges may be "embarked in a conspiracy with the legislature," Hamilton expected the people to be "enlightened enough to distinguish between a legal exercise and an illegal usurpation of authority."

James Madison says in Federalist Paper No. 44, last paragraph:

> "In the first instance, the success of the usurpation will depend on the executive and judiciary departments, which are to expound and give effect to the legislative acts; and in the last resort a remedy must be obtained from the people who can, by the election of more faithful representatives, annul the acts of the usurpers."

The founders expected the people to be the natural guardians of the Constitution, and to take whatever action is necessary when their representatives in the federal government concur with the usurpations of another Branch thereby violating their oaths to preserve the Constitution.

What about filing lawsuits?

Not one founder advocated filing lawsuits as a remedy. Over time it has become evident by the court opinions that many courts are not aligned with the original intentions of the founders or the Constitution, which commits to protect the natural rights of ordinary citizens.

Exceptions Clause

Article III establishes the federal courts. Section 2 of that article enumerates the categories of cases which federal courts are allowed to hear and distributes the authority to hear cases between the Supreme Court and the lower federal courts.

In two of the categories of cases enumerated in Article III, Section 2, the Constitution grants original trial jurisdiction to the Supreme Court for (1) all cases affecting ambassadors, other public ministers and consuls, and (2) those in which a state is a party. In all other enumerated categories of cases "the supreme Court shall have appellate Jurisdiction, both as to Law and Fact, with such Exceptions, and under such Regulations as the Congress shall make."

Some, including some law professors, say the phrase means that Congress may extend the Supreme Court's original (trial) jurisdiction to include more cases than just those two enumerated cases. That view is incorrect. Congress may not unilaterally amend the Constitution by expanding the Supreme Court's "original" jurisdiction.

Others say the phrase means that Congress may withdraw from the federal court's authority to hear certain types of cases. That is also incorrect. It is true that the federal courts have been hearing cases which they are not authorized by Article III, Section 2, to hear, but the remedy for that is impeachment and removal of the usurping judges. The "exceptions clause" does not permit Congress to diminish the enumerated powers of the federal courts. That would take an amendment, not an opinion.

What does the clause mean?

Hamilton tells us in Federalist Paper No. 81. The quoted phrase merely addresses technical issues respecting the method of appeals: Will the appeal be heard by a jury or by judges? Will the appellate court be able to revisit matters of fact? Or will it be restricted to reviewing rulings on matters of law? Will the method of appeals be the same for cases involving the common law and the civil law or will it be different for each?

Congress will decide.

Jurisdiction Explained

Can the federal courts override your state laws? Do they have jurisdiction?

Illegal immigration numbers have steadily and sharply increased in southwestern states, especially Arizona, in recent years. As a result, in April 2010, Arizona enacted two laws which address immigration, SB 1070 and HB 2162. These laws added new state requirements, crimes, and penalties related to enforcement of immigration laws, and were to become effective on July 29, 2010.

Before the laws could go into effect, the U.S. Department of Justice filed a lawsuit which asked for an injunction against these laws by arguing that they are unconstitutional.

Arizona Governor Jan Brewer appealed the injunction and arguments were heard by the 9th U.S. Circuit Court of Appeals, which is a lower federal court on Nov. 1, 2010. On April 11, 2011, the court upheld the injunction.

The only legitimate question: Does the Arizona law violate the U.S. Constitution? The answer to that question is "No."

The supremacy clause of the Constitution, Article VI, clause 2, states:

> "This Constitution, and the Laws of the United States which shall be made in Pursuance thereof; and all Treaties made, or which shall be made, under the authority of the United States, shall be the supreme Law of the Land; and the Judges in every State shall be bound thereby, any Thing in the Constitution or Laws of any State to the Contrary notwithstanding."

Note the wording, for therein is the answer to the question.

Only laws made by Congress which are pursuant to the Constitution qualify as part of the supreme law of the land.

Alexander Hamilton says in Federalist Paper No. 27, last paragraph:

> "It merits particular attention in this place, that the laws of the Confederacy, as to the ENUMERATED and LEGITIMATE objects of its jurisdiction, will become the SUPREME LAW of the land; to the observance of which all officers, legislative, executive, and judicial, in each State, will be bound by the sanctity of an oath. Thus the legislatures, courts, and magistrates, of the respective members, will be incorporated into the operations of the national government AS FAR AS ITS JUST AND CONSTITUTIONAL AUTHORITY EXTENDS; and will be rendered auxiliary to the enforcement of its laws."

In Federalist Paper No. 33, 7th paragraph, Hamilton says:

> "But it will not follow from this doctrine that acts of the large society which are NOT PURSUANT to its constitutional powers, but which are invasions of the residuary authorities of the smaller societies, will become the supreme law of the land. These will be merely acts of usurpation, and will deserve to be treated as such."

When Congress makes laws which are not within its enumerated powers, such laws are mere acts of usurpation and do not have supremacy over anything.

Article VI, clause 2, also shows that only laws of states which are contrary to the Constitution must fall. States may make whatever laws they wish, consistent with their state Constitutions, except in those few instance cited in Article I, Section 10, of the Constitution which are prohibited.

States also may not create laws which contradict the Constitution. For example, a state law which permits people as young as 25 years old to be U.S. Senators contradicts Article I, Section 3, clause 3, and would fail under the supremacy clause.

When a state law is not contrary to the Constitution, nor contradicts it, then the state law remains in full force and effect and is not affected by the supremacy clause.

Now consider exclusive jurisdiction, those few matters in which the federal government has sole authority to act. When our Constitution bestows sole authority on the federal government, then any state law to the contrary would fall.

Hamilton explains this in Federalist No. 32, 2nd paragraph:

> "But as the plan of the convention aims only at a partial union or consolidation, the State governments would clearly retain all the rights of sovereignty which they before had, and which were not, by that act, EXCLUSIVELY delegated to the United States. This exclusive delegation, or rather this alienation, of State sovereignty, would only exist in three cases:"

Hamilton then describes the three cases where the Constitution grants to the federal government sole authority to act:

- Where the Constitution expressly grants an exclusive authority to the federal government; as in Article I, Section. 8, next to last clause, which grants to Congress the power to "exercise exclusive Legislation in all Cases whatsoever," over the District of Columbia, military forts, dockyards, and other needful buildings.
- Where it grants an authority to the federal government, and prohibits the states from exercising that same authority; as in Article I, Section 8, clause 1, which authorizes Congress "To lay and collect Taxes, Duties, Imposts and Excises," combined with Article I, Section 10, clause 2, which declares that, "No State shall, without the Consent of the Congress, lay any Imposts or Duties on Imports or Exports..."

- Where it grants an authority to the federal government, "to which a similar authority in the States would be absolutely and totally CONTRADICTORY and REPUGNANT" as Alexander Hamilton stated in Federalist Paper No. 32. Article I, Section 8, clause 4, declares that Congress shall have power "to establish an uniform rule of naturalization throughout the United States." This must necessarily be exclusive because if each state had power to prescribe a distinct rule, there could not be a uniform rule.

These three examples are the only cases where the federal government has exclusive authority. In all other matters within the enumerated powers, the federal and state governments have concurrent jurisdiction. This is where the Constitution authorizes the federal government to act and does not prohibit the states from acting on the same matter.

A good example is Article I, Section 8, clause 7, which authorizes the federal government to deliver our mail when it says Congress shall have the power "to establish Post Offices and post Roads." but does not prohibit the states or the people from doing so. Accordingly, we have private companies such as FedEx and UPS that compete with the federal government in the delivery of mail. In those cases, the federal government and the states have a concurrent and coequal authority as Hamilton explained in Federalist Paper No. 32.

Might there be conflicts when both the federal government and state governments are acting on the same matter? Yes. Hamilton pointed out in subsequent paragraphs:

> "It is not, however a mere possibility of inconvenience in the exercise of powers, but an immediate constitutional repugnancy that can by implication alienate and extinguish a pre-existing right of sovereignty.
>
> The necessity of a concurrent jurisdiction in certain cases results from the division of the sovereign power; and the rule that all authorities, of which the States are not explicitly divested in favor of the Union, remain with

them in full vigor, is not a theoretical consequence of that division, but is clearly admitted by the whole tenor of the instrument which contains the articles of the proposed Constitution. We there find that, notwithstanding the affirmative grants of general authorities, there has been the most pointed care in those cases where it was deemed improper that the like authorities should reside in the States, to insert negative clauses prohibiting the exercise of them by the States. The tenth section of the first article consists altogether of such provisions."

Even where the Constitution delegates a power to the federal government, the sovereign states retain a concurrent and coequal authority over the same matter unless the Constitution specifically prohibits the states from exercising that power.

Now let us look at Article I, Section 8, clause 4. The Congress shall have power, "To establish an uniform Rule of Naturalization..."

James Madison explains in Federalist Paper No. 42, 5th paragraph, the reason for the clause. Under the Articles of Confederation, the various states had their own rules for qualifying for citizenship:

"By the laws of several States, certain descriptions of aliens, who had rendered themselves obnoxious, were laid under interdicts inconsistent not only with the rights of citizenship but with the privilege of residence. What would have been the consequence, if such persons, by residence or otherwise, had acquired the character of citizens under the laws of another State, and then asserted their rights as such, both to residence and citizenship, within the State proscribing them? Whatever the legal consequences might have been, other consequences would probably have resulted, of too serious a nature not to be provided against. The new Constitution has accordingly, with great propriety, made provision against them, and all others proceeding from the defect of the Confederation on this head, by authorizing the general government to

establish a uniform rule of naturalization throughout the
United States.

This clause in the Constitution grants the federal government exclusive
authority to set the *criteria* for citizenship. The only way Arizona could
violate Article I, Section. 8, clause 4, would be if Arizona made a law
which purported to set different criteria for citizenship in Arizona.

Does the Arizona law set different criteria for citizenship?

When Arizona officials make lawful contact with illegal aliens, they turn
them over to the custody of the federal government. Arizona officials
propose to turn these illegal aliens over to the United States Immigration
and Customs Enforcement (ICE) or to the United States Customs and
Border Protection. That does not establish different criteria for citizenship.

Other provisions of the Arizona law address crimes committed by
illegal aliens and others within the borders of the state such as criminal
trespass, human smuggling, impeding traffic while picking up day
laborers, harboring and concealing illegal aliens, and knowingly
employing illegal aliens. After the illegal aliens have served their
sentences, they will be turned over to ICE or U.S. Customs and Border
Protection. This does not set different criteria for citizenship.

Where is the conflict with the Constitution? How does the Arizona law
violate the Constitution for officials of the sovereign state of Arizona to
turn illegal aliens over to the federal authorities?

Alexander Hamilton shows in Federalist Paper No. 32 the proper
questions to ask.

Is there anything in the U.S. Constitution which makes the powers
asserted by the sovereign state of Arizona exclusive in the federal
government? Is there anything in the U.S. Constitution which prohibits
the states from exercising the powers which Arizona exercises in her law?

In fact, it is Arizona which has exclusive jurisdiction over illegal aliens
who commit violations of Arizona's criminal laws, and the federal

government does not have any authority to interfere. To the extent the federal government does interfere, its actions would not be pursuant to the Constitution. Those actions of interference would be mere usurpations of power and would deserve to be treated as such.

There is nothing in the U.S. Constitution which prohibits Arizona from exercising the powers in her law. So far is this from being the case, that a plain and conclusive argument to the contrary is to be deduced from Article I, Section 10, last clause:

> "No State shall, with the Consent of Congress, lay any Duty of Tonnage, keep Troops, or Ships of War in time of Peace, enter into any Agreement or Compact with another State, or with a foreign Power, or engage in War, unless actually invaded, or in such imminent danger as will not admit of delay."

There is nothing in the above clause of the Constitution, or anywhere else in the Constitution, which prohibits Arizona from turning illegal aliens over to the custody of the federal authorities.

There is nothing in the above clause of the Constitution, or anywhere else in the Constitution, which prohibits the state from prosecuting illegal aliens for their crimes which were committed within the borders of that state.

There is nothing in the above clause of the Constitution, or anywhere else in the Constitution, which prohibits the state of Arizona from keeping troops and engaging in war to defend against an invasion of illegal aliens.

It has been shown before that Article IV, Section 4, requires the federal government to protect each of the states against invasion. The founders gave the federal government every tool possible to defend the country from invasions, even to the point of authorizing the borrowing money to get it done. But if the federal government refuses to do its duty, then the sovereign states have both a natural and an expressed authority to do it themselves.

THE HANDBOOK FOR WE THE PEOPLE

Related Questions and Research Assignments

1. Reading assignment: Read Article IV.

2. Paraphrase the following segment of Alexander Hamilton's Federalist Paper No. 83:

> "In like manner the judicial authority of the federal judicatures is declared by the Constitution to comprehend certain cases particularly specified. The expression of those cases marks the precise limits, beyond which the federal courts cannot extend their jurisdiction, because the objects of their cognizance being enumerated, the specification would be nugatory if it did not exclude all ideas of more extensive authority."

3. Paraphrase the following segment of Alexander Hamilton's Federalist Paper No. 80:

> "It seems scarcely to admit of controversy, that the judicary authority of the Union ought to extend to these several descriptions of cases: 1st, to all those which arise out of the laws of the United States, passed in pursuance of their just and constitutional powers of legislation; 2d, to all those which concern the execution of the provisions expressly contained in the articles of Union; 3d, to all those in which the United States are a party; 4th, to all those which involve the PEACE of the CONFEDERACY, whether they relate to the intercourse between the United States and foreign nations, or to that between the States themselves; 5th, to all those which originate on the high seas, and are of admiralty or maritime jurisdiction; and, lastly, to all those in which the State tribunals cannot be supposed to be impartial and unbiased."

4. Research the three famous Supreme Court cases below and explain why the Supreme Court opinions are contrary to the Constitution and the principles found in the Declaration of Independence. Use original sources only.

   A. The Dred Scott Case.
   B. Korematsu versus United States.
   C. Wickard versus Filburn.

5. Some judges have stated that they have the right to make policy from the bench. Research and give examples of quotes of at least two Supreme Court judges. How would you support or refute their opinions using the Constitution?

6. Does the Supreme Court of the U.S. have jurisdiction if Congress has passed a law not covered by the enumerated powers? Explain.

7. What argument could you present to someone who says we have *constitutional* rights to this or that subject?

8. Do you think universal moral restraints exist? If so, what might some of them be? How do these coincide with "natural" rights?

9. How has the original intent of the 14th Amendment been changed?

10. Research "Rule of Law" versus "Rule of Man." What is the difference between the two? Which would you prefer to live under and why?

Chapter 6

NULLIFICATION

"I should like merely to understand how it happens that so many men, so many villages, so many cities, so many nations, sometimes suffer under a single tyrant who has no other power than the power they gave him; who is able to harm them only to the extent to which they have the willingness to bear with him; who could do them absolutely no injury unless they preferred to put up with him rather than contradict him."

These are the words of a 14th century French writer and philosopher by the name of Etienne de La Boetie in his essay, *The Politics of Obedience*. Mr. La Boetie understood the natural right of nullification at an early age.

Nullification simply means "We refuse to do it."

When the federal government usurps power and acts in a tyrannical manner toward the states or the people, what did our framers really say we that must do?

Recommendations did not include filing lawsuits or amending the constitution. There is a distinction to be made between abuses of *delegated* powers and usurpations of powers which have not been delegated.

The framers advised two remedies: nullification and the election of more faithful and virtuous representatives.

For usurpations of powers which have not been delegated and are outside the lawful reach of the federal government, like health care, then nullification is the proper answer according to Madison, Hamilton, and Jefferson.

An example of the abuse of delegated powers would be unwise bankruptcy laws as authorized in Article. I, Section 8, clause 4, for which election of better representatives is the answer.

In order to understand the right of nullification, we must refer back to the founding principles set forth in the Declaration of Independence, second paragraph. These founding principles are:

- Our rights are unalienable and come from God.
- The purpose of civil government is to protect our God-given rights.
- Civil government is legitimate only when it operates with our consent.
- Since the U.S. Constitution forms the federal civil government, it operates with our consent only when it obeys the Constitution. When it does not obey the Constitution and takes away any of our natural rights, we have the right and the duty to alter, abolish, or throw off such government.

Many volumes of books and articles have been written on the subject of state nullification to explain what the founders intended and what they did not.

Many well-respected folks say that nullification by states of unconstitutional acts of the federal government is unlawful and/or impossible.

These same highly regarded folks appear unaware of the two conditions which our framers said must be present before nullification is proper and possible.

1. The act of the federal government must be unconstitutional, usually a usurpation of a power not delegated to the federal government in the Constitution.

2. The act must be something the states or the people can refuse to obey. The act must order them to do, or not do something. How is it possible to say you are not going to do something if you are not required to do it in the first place?

Here are three illustrations showing when nullification is or is not an option:

1. When the act of the federal government is unconstitutional and orders the states or the people to do, or not do, something, then nullification is the proper form of interposition.

   Laws which require citizens to register arms, laws which prohibit students from praying at school, and laws that force citizens to purchase health insurance are not subjects which Congress has any authority to address for the nation as a whole. In addition, they require the states or the people to act or not act so both requirements are fulfilled.

2. When the act of the federal government is unconstitutional, but does not order the states or the people to do or not do something, as in the Alien and Sedition Acts, nullification is not possible. The states may interpose by objecting, as in The Virginia and Kentucky Resolutions of 1798.

3. When the act of the federal government is constitutional, but unjust, such as the Tariff Act of 1828, the states may not nullify it. But the states may interpose by objecting and trying to get the legislation changed.

   When any branch of the federal government steps outside the Constitution to make laws, rules, orders, or opinions which exceed their delegated powers, the states must resort to those original rights which predate and preexist our constitution to nullify such usurpations by the federal government of non-delegated powers.

Some, who claim to be experts, make demonstrably false assertions concerning the act of nullification and say:

- States do not have the right to nullify unconstitutional acts of the federal government because our Constitution does not say they can.
- Nullification is literally impossible.
- The Supreme Court is the final authority on what is constitutional and what is not; and the states and the people must submit to whatever the Supreme Court says.
- James Madison, "Father of the Constitution," opposed nullification.

These assertions contradict our Declaration of Independence, The Federalist Papers, our federal Constitution, and what James Madison, Thomas Jefferson, and Alexander Hamilton really said.

Each assertion is listed below and countered by using original source documents.

1. The states cannot nullify unconstitutional acts of the federal government because the Constitution does not say they can do it.

   As Madison says in his Notes on Nullification (1834), one can see that "when powers are assumed which have not been delegated, a nullification of the act" is a "natural right."

   The framers regarded the right of nullification as one with the hallowed status of a natural right of self-defense, not as a paltry constitutional right that could be decided by the courts. It applies to every single state, county, parish, city, town, and citizen.

   Thomas Jefferson said in the Kentucky Resolutions of 1798:

   > "...but where powers are assumed which have not been delegated, a nullification of the act is the rightful remedy: that every State has a natural right

in cases not within the compact,...to nullify of their own authority all assumptions of power by others within their limits: that without this right, they would be under the dominion, absolute and unlimited, of whosoever might exercise this right of judgment for them..."

James Madison commented on Mr. Jefferson's statement above in his Notes on Nullification (1834), near the end:

"...the right of nullification meant by Mr. Jefferson is the natural right, which all admit to be a remedy against insupportable oppression..."

Alexander Hamilton says in Federalist Paper No. 28, 6th paragraph:

"If the representatives of the people betray their constituents, there is then no resource left but in the exertion of that original right of self-defense which is paramount to all positive forms of government, and which against the usurpations of the national rulers, may be exerted with infinitely better prospect of success than against those of the rulers of an individual state."

Hamilton then shows that the states can rein in a usurping federal government:

"It may safely be received as an axiom in our political system, that the State governments will, in all possible contingencies, afford complete security against invasions of the public liberty by the national authority."

But the nullification opponents do not agree, so they reject, or do not understand, the founding principle that natural rights predate and preexist the Constitution and come from God.

The natural right of nullification transcends the Constitution and, since it is not prohibited by the Constitution to the states, is a reserved power as the 10th Amendment affirms.

Nothing in the federal Constitution prohibits the states from nullifying unconstitutional acts of the federal government.

We saw where Madison said in Federalist Paper No. 45 that the powers delegated to the federal government are few and defined, and all other powers are reserved to the several states.

Therefore, nullification is a reserved power of the states and the people. The only way a state could not lawfully nullify unconstitutional federal acts is if an individual state Constitution specifically prohibited it.

The states do not go to the Constitution to look for permission because they retain all the powers they did not exclusively delegate to the federal government.

It is the federal government which is supposed to look to the Constitution for permission to address a subject, not the states. This is an opposite view from the nullification opponents.

As we have just seen, Jefferson, Madison, and Hamilton saw nullification of unconstitutional acts of the federal government as a natural right, not a constitutional right. Since rights come from God, there is no such thing as a constitutional right of nullification in the U.S. Constitution.

2. Nullification of unconstitutional federal legislation is literally impossible.

We saw above the two conditions which must exist before nullification is possible, according to the framers, the Declaration of Independence, and The Federalist Papers:

- The act of the federal government must be unconstitutional.

- The act must be something the people or the states can refuse to obey.

Here are examples of unconstitutional federal acts which may be nullified because they fulfill the two requirements above:

A. The Constitution does not delegate to the federal government power to address the subject of religion, either for it or against it for the nation as a whole. But in 1962, the Supreme Court first ordered the states to stop prayers in the public schools. That Supreme Court next banned the Ten Commandments from the public schools.

Since those orders were usurpations of powers not lawfully possessed by the Supreme Court, the states could have nullified them by directing their school boards to ignore them.

B. If Congress by law, or the president by executive order, orders the people to turn in their guns, they have the natural right to refuse to comply. The Constitution does not authorize the federal government to disarm the citizens. The states and the people can nullify such law or order by refusing to obey.

C. In like manner, the people may nullify unconstitutional and unjust state and municipal laws as well. The Jim Crow laws required black people to sit at the back of the bus, and prohibited them from eating in public places and using public restrooms, water fountains, park benches, etc. Using nonviolent civil disobedience, Rosa Parks and Martin Luther King led black people to refuse to obey these unjust and unconstitutional laws as affirmed in the first section of the 14th Amendment. This was nullification by citizens.

The following is an example of unconstitutional acts which could not be nullified because they were not directed to anything the states or the people could refuse to obey: The Alien and Sedition Acts.

In 1798 Thomas Jefferson wrote The Kentucky Resolutions, and James Madison wrote The Virginia Resolutions. These resolutions objected, as opposed to nullified, laws made by Congress which purported to grant to the president dictatorial powers over alien and seditious words.

Kentucky and Virginia could *object*, but they couldn't prevent the president from enforcing the Alien and Sedition Acts, because the president had the raw power to arrest and prosecute aliens or people who had spoken or written seditious words.

Jefferson and Madison showed in the resolutions why the Alien and Sedition Acts were unconstitutional as a result and protested them and asked other states to join the protest.

The two paragraphs in the Virginia Resolutions which some cite as the reference as to the states' lack of literal power to nullify anything as to the ultimate authority of the Judicial Branch, appear under Madison's discussion of the last two resolutions where Virginia had asked other states to join the protest. Madison writes that the citizens and legislature of Virginia have the right to communicate with other states and by doing so they are not exercising a judicial function.

Madison actually writes in the same report that the experts cite, that it is "a plain principle, founded in common sense" that the states are the final authority on whether the federal government has violated our Constitution. In the Virginia Resolutions, under his discussion of the third resolution, Madison says:

> "It appears to your committee to be a plain principle, founded in common sense, illustrated by common practice, and essential to the nature of compacts; that where resort can be had to no tribunal superior to the authority of the parties, the parties themselves

must be the rightful judges in the last resort, whether the bargain made, has been pursued or violated. The Constitution of the United States was formed by the sanction of the States, given by each in its sovereign capacity. It adds to the stability and dignity, as well as to the authority of the Constitution, that it rests on this legitimate and solid foundation. The States then being the parties to the constitutional compact, and in their sovereign capacity, it follows of necessity, that there can be no tribunal above their authority, to decide in the last resort, whether the compact made by them be violated; and consequently that as the parties to it, they must themselves decide in the last resort, such questions as may be of sufficient magnitude to require their interposition."

A bit farther down, Madison explains that if, when the federal government usurps power, the states cannot act so as to stop the usurpation, and thereby preserve the Constitution as well as the safety of the states, there would be no relief from usurped power. This would subvert the rights of the people as well as betray the fundamental principle of our founding:

"...If the deliberate exercise, of dangerous power, palpably withheld by the Constitution, could not justify the parties to it, in interposing even so far as to arrest the progress of the evil, and thereby to preserve the Constitution itself as well as to provide for the safety of the parties to it; there would be an end to all relief from usurped power, and a direct subversion of the rights specified or recognized under all the State constitutions, as well as a plain denial of the fundamental principle on which our independence itself was declared."

Farther down, Madison answers the objection of convention members "that the judicial authority is to be regarded as the sole expositor of the Constitution, in the last resort."

Madison explains that when the federal government acts outside the Constitution by usurping powers, and when the Constitution affords no remedy to that usurpation, then the sovereign states who are the parties to the Constitution must likewise step outside the Constitution and appeal to that original natural right of self-defense.

Madison also says that the Judicial Branch is as likely to usurp as are the other two branches. Thus the sovereign states, as the parties to the Constitution, have as much right to judge the usurpations of the Judicial Branch as they do the Legislative and Executive Branches:

> "...the judicial department, also, may exercise or sanction dangerous powers beyond the grant of the Constitution; and, consequently, that the ultimate right of the parties to the Constitution, to judge whether the compact has been dangerously violated, must extend to violations by one delegated authority as well as by another, by the judiciary as well as by the executive, or the legislature."

Madison goes on to say that all three branches of the federal government obtain their delegated powers from the Constitution, and they may not annul the authority of their Creator. If the Judicial Branch connives with other branches in usurping powers, our Constitution will be destroyed. So the Judicial Branch does not have final say:

> "...to the rights of the parties to the constitutional compact, from which the judicial as well as the other department hold their delegated trusts. On any other hypothesis, the delegation of judicial power, would annul the authority delegating it and the concurrence of this department with the others in usurped powers, might subvert forever, and beyond the possible reach of any rightful remedy, the very Constitution, which all were instituted to preserve."

3. The Supreme Court is the final authority on what is constitutional and what is not while the states and the people must submit to whatever the Supreme Court says.

Under this assertion, the federal government we created with the Constitution is the exclusive and final judge of the extent of the powers which we delegated to it. The opinion of five judges, not the Constitution, is the sole measure of its powers.

Under the view of some experts, only Congress can correct Congress, and only the federal courts may correct the federal courts.

According to all of the above original sources, Madison's position was misrepresented when it was said he advocated that the Judicial Branch is the final authority.

4. James Madison opposed nullification by states of unconstitutional acts of the federal government.

Not true.

What Madison said was that South Carolina cannot nullify a *constitutional* act. Of course Madison opposed South Carolina's peculiar doctrine of nullification. Madison, along with Jefferson and Hamilton, said the nullified act must be unconstitutional.

There is a distinction between the nullification doctrine which Madison, Jefferson, and Hamilton embraced and the peculiar doctrine of nullification advanced by South Carolina.

We saw in Madison's Report on the Virginia Resolutions (1799-1800) that in a proper case, "interposing even so far as to arrest the progress of the evil" is essential "to preserve the Constitution itself as well as to provide for the safety of the parties to it."

We saw above that the condition which must be present before nullification is deemed proper is that the act of the federal government must be unconstitutional.

Consider The Tariff Act of 1828 and the South Carolina nullification crisis.

A brief review of history shows South Carolina was an agricultural state. During the 1820's, they bought manufactured goods from England. England, in turn, bought cotton produced by South Carolina and other southern states.

However, infant industries in the northeast produced some of the same manufactured goods as England, but they were more expensive than the English imports and were not able to compete with England's cheaper imports.

In 1828, Congress imposed a high tariff on the English imports. The southern states called this the "tariff of abominations" because the tariff made the English goods too expensive to buy. Since the southern states stopped buying English goods, the English stopped buying southern cotton. The southern states had to pay more for manufactured goods, they lost the major buyer of their cotton, and their economy was weakened.

Our Constitution delegates specific authority to Congress to impose tariffs on imports, and the tariff must be the same in each state as stated in Article I, Section 8, clause 1.

Therefore, the Tariff Act of 1828 was constitutional.

South Carolina wanted to nullify a constitutional law.

South Carolina's House of Representatives immediately set forth their doctrine to nullify the Tariff Act of 1828 asserting that:

1. A state has a constitutional right to nullify any federal law.

2. The nullification is presumed valid, and is to remain in force, unless three-fourths of the states, in a convention, say the nullification is not valid.

What Madison said in his Notes on Nullification (1834) was the particular doctrine of nullification set forth by South Carolina did not recognize:

- The federal government has delegated authority to impose import tariffs.
- The Constitution requires that all import tariffs be uniform throughout the United States.
- States cannot nullify tariffs which are authorized by the Constitution.
- One fourth of the states do not have the right to dictate to the rest of the states on matters within the powers delegated to the federal government.
- Nullification is not a paltry constitutional right.

Near the end of his Notes, Madison quoted Thomas Jefferson's Statement:

"...but, where powers are assumed which have not been delegated, a nullification of the act is the rightful remedy: that every State has a natural right in cases not within the compact, (casus non foederis,) to nullify of their own authority all assumptions of power by others within their limits: that without this right, they would be under the dominion, absolute and unlimited, of whosoever might exercise this right of judgment for them..."

Madison then writes:

"Thus the right of nullification meant by Mr. Jefferson is the natural right, which all admit to be a remedy against insupportable oppression."

How is this applicable today?

When We the People ratified our Constitution, and thereby created the federal government, we did not delegate to our creature power to regulate:

- Medical care.
- Energy.
- Guns and ammunition.
- Funding of unconstitutional federal programs.
- Public schools.
- How we use our lands.
- The thousands of other things that the federal government has assumed the authority to do.

Each state has a natural right to nullify these unconstitutional dictates within its borders. As Jefferson and Madison said, without nullification, the states and the people would be under the absolute and unlimited control of the federal government.

In Federalist Paper No. 46, Madison writes with respect to unconstitutional acts of the federal government:

- The people can refuse to cooperate with federal officers.
- State officials can oppose the federal officers.
- State legislatures can invent legislative devices to impede and obstruct the federal government.
- States can cooperate in concerted plans of resistance.

As the last resort, states must defend themselves from the federal government. That is why the people are armed.

To sum this up:

Nullification is a natural right of self-defense.

Right of nullification does not come from the Constitution. Like all rights, the right of self-defense comes from God and is affirmed in the

Declaration of Independence, second paragraph, which affirms the people's right to overthrow tyrannical government.

Nullification is a reserved power within the meaning of the 10th Amendment. The Constitution does not prohibit states from nullifying, and we reserved the power to do it.

Nullification is required by the oath of office, Article VI, clause 3 as it requires all state officers and judges to "support" the federal Constitution. Therefore, when the federal government violates the Constitution, the states have the duty to nullify.

A short word about jury nullification.

Assume that you have been summoned for jury duty ("petty jury") for a trial in federal court. Here are a few things you need to know.

Article III, Section 2, clause 1, shows that the federal courts are granted permission to hear several categories of cases. You may be called to be a juror in either a criminal case or a civil case. A criminal case would most likely involve an alleged violation of the federal criminal code. A civil case would most likely involve a case between citizens residing in different states over some non-criminal issue as breach of contract, negligence, etc.

The issue of jury nullification arises in criminal cases where the defendant is charged with an unjust, unfair, or unconstitutional federal law such as the "crime" of failing to buy health insurance.

Article III, Section 2, last clause, says:

> "The Trial of all Crimes, except in Cases of Impeachment, shall be by Jury..."

Note the entry for "Jury" in Webster's 1828 Dictionary:

> "Petty juries, consisting usually of twelve men, attend courts to try matters of fact in civil cases, and to decide both the law and the fact in criminal prosecutions."

According to the above definition, when the Constitution was ratified, our framers understood that jurors had the right to decide the law in criminal trials. This means that the jurors have the right to judge the law. If you find the law unreasonable, unconstitutional, unfairly applied, or that the defendant has been unfairly singled out, then you have the right and the duty, in a criminal case to find the defendant not guilty.

Alexander Hamilton, a lawyer, was well aware of the problem of unjust criminal statutes. He writes in Federalist Paper No. 83, 12th paragraph:

> "...arbitrary methods of prosecuting pretended offenses, and arbitrary punishments upon arbitrary convictions, have ever appeared to me to be the great engines of judicial despotism; and these have all relation to criminal proceedings."

The overriding issue is even if the Prosecutor proves beyond a reasonable doubt that the defendant failed to buy health insurance, do you, as a Juror, have the right or the duty to refuse conviction? The prosecutor and the judge may insist that you do not have that right. In fact, the judge is likely to instruct you that if you find, as a matter of fact, that the defendant failed to buy health insurance, then you must find him guilty.

Defense counsel may want to tell you the judge is not correct. He may want to tell you about your right and your duty of jury nullification. But judges do not allow defense counsel to so inform you. They may order defense counsel to jail for contempt before they can tell you.

If you, as a juror, find the law unfair, unreasonable, unconstitutional, unfairly applied, or that the defendant has been unfairly singled out or treated, then you have the right—the duty—to find the defendant not guilty.

The judge will probably require you to take an oath that you will follow the law as she or he explains it to you. If you find that the defendant violated the statute, then you must find him guilty. If you say anything about "judging the law" or "is the statute under which defendant is charged constitutional," then the prosecutor will take you off the jury. However, both counsels have the right to ask you questions during a preliminary examination of a witness or a juror to determine whether you will be a good juror for their side. You are under oath to tell the truth when you are questioned. So, if the prosecutor asks you about "Jury Nullification," do you know about it? Do you agree with it? You must tell the truth. Otherwise, you could be tried for perjury. You have the right, when you take the juror's oath in a federal criminal case, to assume that the judge is fair, impartial, and will obey the Constitution since she or he took an oath to do so. Once you are seated in the jury box, find out what the defendant is charged with, hear the evidence, go into the jury room to deliberate, you must do as your conscience dictates.

Related Questions and Research Assignments

1. Read both the Kentucky and Virginia Resolutions of 1798 in their entirety shown in the back of this book.

2. Paraphrase the following segment of Alexander Hamilton's Federalist Paper No. 28:

> "If the representatives of the people betray their constituents, there is then no resource left but in the exertion of that original right of self-defense which is paramount to all positive forms of government, and which against the usurpations of the national rulers, may be exerted with infinitely better prospect of success than against those of the rulers of an individual State. In a single State, if the persons intrusted with supreme power become usurpers, the different parcels, subdivisions, or districts of which it consists, having no distinct government in each, can take no regular measures for defense. The citizens must rush tumultuously to arms, without concert, without system, without resource; except in their courage and despair. The usurpers, clothed with the forms of legal authority, can too often crush the opposition in embryo. The smaller the extent of the territory, the more difficult will it be for the people to form a regular or systematic plan of opposition, and the more easy will it be to defeat their early efforts. Intelligence can be more speedily obtained of their preparations and movements, and the military force in the possession of the usurpers can be more rapidly directed against the part where the opposition has begun. In this situation there must be a peculiar coincidence of circumstances to insure success to the popular resistance."

3. Paraphrase the following segment of James Madison's Federalist Paper No. 39:

> "But if the government be national with regard to the OPERATION of its powers, it changes its aspect again when we contemplate it in relation to the EXTENT of its powers. The idea of a national government involves in it, not only an authority over the individual citizens, but an indefinite supremacy over all persons and things, so far as they are objects of lawful government. Among a people consolidated into one nation, this supremacy is completely vested in the national legislature. Among communities united for particular purposes, it is vested partly in the general and partly in the municipal legislatures. In the former case, all local authorities are subordinate to the supreme; and may be controlled, directed, or abolished by it at pleasure. In the latter, the local or municipal authorities form distinct and independent portions of the supremacy, no more subject, within their respective spheres, to the general authority, than the general authority is subject to them, within its own sphere. In this relation, then, the proposed government cannot be deemed a NATIONAL one; since its jurisdiction extends to certain enumerated objects only, and leaves to the several States a residuary and inviolable sovereignty over all other objects. It is true that in controversies relating to the boundary between the two jurisdictions, the tribunal which is ultimately to decide, is to be established under the general government. But this does not change the principle of the case. The decision is to be impartially made, according to the rules of the Constitution; and all the usual and most effectual precautions are taken to secure this impartiality. Some such tribunal is clearly essential to prevent an appeal to the sword and a dissolution of the compact; and that it ought to be established under the general rather than under the local governments, or, to speak more properly, that it could be

safely established under the first alone, is a position not likely to be combated."

4. What factors must be present in order for a state to nullify federal laws?

5. Based on the Constitution, and the founders, why is nullification a legitimate action which can be taken by a state or states under certain conditions?

6. How is nullification related to the natural rights of self-defense?

7. Are the states obligated to nullify unconstitutional acts by the federal government? Why or why not?

Chapter 7

GOD, CHURCH, AND STATE

Many books have been written about the link between our nation's beginnings to the Creator and how the founders framed the Constitution around God's model of politics. The study of strict construction, however, leads us in an additional direction.

Recently, our country has become a land where Christian children are forbidden to use the word God in the public schools. Our country has become a place where public school students are forbidden to say prayers at football games, and a place where Christian religious speech is banned from the public square.

This chapter will explain how judges on the Supreme Court justified their decisions contrary to the Constitution, prohibited the free exercise of religion, and abridged our freedom of speech.

What does our Constitution say, or not say, about religion and speech?

Since religion and speech are not among the enumerated powers specifically listed in the Constitution, Congress may not make any laws either for or against the subject of religion or speech.

Furthermore, the First Amendment to the Constitution says:

> "Congress shall make no law respecting an establishment
> of religion, or prohibiting the free exercise thereof; or
> abridging the freedom of speech..."

Since this is the case, where did judges get the authority to hear cases on religion and speech?

Judges on the Supreme Court changed the historical definition of the term "established" religion which, in turn, enabled them to decide cases on the subject of religion.

But first, what is an established religion as the founders understood it?

We will begin by finding out what establishment of religion actually meant when the Constitution was ratified. To do so, we must consult English history, American Colonial history, and the writings of our founders.

Through the study of the many writings and speeches of our framers, an established religion at the time of the founding could be characterized as coercion by the civil government to force the people to practice a specific religion under pain of death, imprisonment and fines, and to financially support the established church.

In the study of the historical aspects of religious freedom as it relates to our founding, consider the following subjects:

- Established religion in England.
- Established religions in the American colonies.
- First Amendment restrictions.
- Bans on the free exercise of religion and abridgment of free speech.
- Redefinition of the historic term *establishment* of religion by the Supreme Court.

Established Religion in England

Queen Mary I, also known as "Bloody Mary," who reigned from 1553 to 1558, deposed the Church of England which her father, Henry VIII, had established. In its place, she re-established the Roman Catholic Church and burned approximately 300 protestant dissenters at stake.

Later, Elizabeth I, who reigned from 1558 to 1603, restored the Church of England. Elizabeth's Act of Uniformity in1559 imposed fines, forfeitures, and imprisonment on church officials who did not conform to approved doctrine and practice. She imposed fines on all persons who, without sufficient excuse, did not attend services of the Church of England.

Then came the reign of Charles II from 1661 to 1685. During his time, the Puritan John Bunyan was imprisoned for eleven years because he refused to attend services of the established Church of England, and he refused to obtain a license to preach as a nonconformist.

The established religions in England, first Roman Catholic, then Church of England, were supported by tithes, which were mandatory payments of a percentage of the produce of the land. The tithes were required by those who lived within the parish, regardless of their religious preferences, to the parish church in order to support it and its clergy.

The payment of tithes was a cause of endless dispute between the tithe owners and the tithe payers, between clergy and parishioners. In addition, Quakers and other nonconformists objected to paying any tithes to support the established church. Almost every agricultural process and product attracted controversy over its tithe value. By the eighteenth century the complex legislation which surrounded the tithe began to have a detrimental effect. Tithing was seen as irrelevant to the needs of the community and the developing agricultural industry.

Established Religions in the American Colonies

As the English settled in the American Colonies along the east coast, they promptly established their religions in accordance to their traditions.

In Massachusetts, where they established the Congregational Church, only church members could vote between 1631 and 1664, dissenters were banished. Between 1650 and 1670, Quakers were whipped, imprisoned, banished, and put to death. Massachusetts also made laws which stayed on the books that directed all Roman Catholics to leave the realm.

In Virginia, where they established the Church of England, penalties for failure to attend services during the early 1600's included death, prison, and fines. In the 1700's, Roman Catholics were forbidden to possess arms, give evidence in court, or hold office unless they took certain oaths. A marriage was not legal unless it was performed by a minister of the Church of England. Everyone in Virginia was required to contribute to the support of the established Church of England, to maintain the building, pay the minister's salary, and provide him with a house and plot of land.

In Maryland, where they established the Church of England, between 1704 and 1775, Roman Catholic services could be held only in private homes. Roman Catholics could not teach school. Inheritance of property by Roman Catholics was restricted, and Roman Catholics who did not take a certain oath were disfranchised and subject to additional taxes, as well as forced to contribute to the established church. Maryland citizens were required to contribute to the support of the established Church of England, to maintain the building, pay the minister's salary, and provide him with a house and plot of land.

North and South Carolina's citizens were also required to contribute to the support of the established Church of England, to maintain the building, pay the minister's salary, and provide him with a house and plot of land.

New York required each county to hire a Protestant minister and to levy taxes for his support.

Rhode Island's laws between 1719 and 1783 prohibited Roman Catholics from being freemen or office holders. Roman Catholics were given full political rights in 1783.

By the late 1700's, things started to change.

In 1760, the Congregational Church was still established in Massachusetts and Connecticut. But Episcopalians, Baptists and Quakers were now tolerated, and were no longer required to support the Congregational Church.

As the spirit of toleration grew in England and colonial America, criminal penalties were abolished for dissenting from the tax-supported established religions.

By 1776, the essential characteristic of established religions, as opposed to tolerated religions, was that the established religions were supported by tax money, or tithes assessed and collected by law, whereas the latter was supported by voluntary contributions alone.

In the process of time when some colonist became Quakers, and some became Baptists, and some returned to the Church of England, objections were made to the mandatory payment of a tax appropriated to the support of a church they had forsaken.

Alexander Hamilton wrote in 1775 in his Remarks on the Quebec Bill, No. 11:

> "The characteristic difference between a tolerated and established religion, consists in this: With respect to the support of the former, the law is passive and improvident, leaving it to those who profess it, to make as much, or as

little, provision as they...judge expedient; and to vary and alter that provision, as their circumstances may require. In this manner, the Presbyterians, and other sects, are tolerated in England. They are allowed to exercise their religion without molestation, and to maintain their clergy as they think proper. These are wholly dependent upon their congregations, and can exact no more than they stipulate and are satisfied to contribute. But with respect to the support of the latter, the law is active and provident. Certain precise dues are legally annexed to the clerical office, independent on the liberal contributions of the people. While tithes were the free gift of the people, the Roman church was only in a state of toleration; but when the law came to take cognizance of them, and, by determining their permanent existence, destroyed the free agency of the people, it then resumed the nature of an establishment."

James Madison wrote in his letter of 1832 to Rev. Adams:

"In the Colonial State of the Country, there were four examples, R.I., N.J., Penna. and Delaware, and the greater part of N.Y. where there were no religious Establishments; the support of Religion being left to the voluntary associations and contributions of individuals..."

Thus the evolution is from established religions to tolerated religions to voluntary religious freedom for the citizens.

First Amendment Restrictions

Before we look at Supreme Court opinions banning the free exercise of religion and abridging free speech, we must consider whose powers are restricted by the First Amendment.

> "Congress shall make no law respecting an establishment of religion, or prohibiting the free exercise thereof; or abridging the freedom of speech..."

The plain language shows that the first amendment restricts only Congress's powers.

The people of the states are free to establish or revoke any religion they want. This is one of the powers retained by the states or the people.

The First Amendment prohibits:

- Congress from establishing a national denominational religion.
- Congress from interfering in the states' establishments of the religions of their choice, or the revoking thereof.
- Congress from abridging the peoples' freedom of speech.

Bans on the Free Exercise of Religion and Abridgment of Free Speech

The judges on the Supreme Court asserted In Gitlow v. People (1925) that the 14th Amendment incorporates the First Amendment so that the First Amendment now restricts the powers of the states. This is known as the incorporation doctrine or "doctrine of incorporation."

The judges' new interpretation of the 14th Amendment has been used to assume power over state and local governments.

On page 666 of the opinion, they wrote:

> "...we may and do assume that freedom of speech and of the press which are protected by the First Amendment from abridgment by Congress are among the fundamental personal rights and "liberties" protected by the due process clause of the Fourteenth Amendment from impairment by the States."

By claiming that the First Amendment restricts the powers of the states and local governments, which it does not, the court set itself up as policeman over the states, over counties, over cities and towns, including football fields and court house lawns.

In this way, the Bill of Rights, which was intended to be the states' and the peoples' protection against usurpations of power by the federal government, had now become the tool the Supreme Court used to usurp power and force their wills on all U.S. citizens.

Redefinition of the Historic Term Establishment of Religion

We have seen that the framers regarded an established religion as one which was supported by mandatory taxes or tithes, whereas tolerated denominations were supported by voluntary offerings of their adherents.

Now let us see how judges on the Supreme Court redefined establishment of religion in order to ban prayer in public schools.

Engel v. Vitale, 1962, is the case where six federal judges outlawed non-denominational prayer in the public schools. A public school board in New York had directed that the following prayer be said at school:

> "Almighty God, we acknowledge our dependence upon
> Thee, and we beg Thy blessings upon us, our parents, our
> teachers and our Country."

Any student was free to remain seated or leave the room without any comments by the teacher one way or the other.

Six judges on the Supreme Court said in their opinion that this short non-denominational and voluntary prayer constituted an establishment of religion in violation of the First Amendment.

In order to rule on the subject of religion which is prohibited to the federal courts, these judges had to redefine the establishment of religion so they could issue opinions on the subject.

They redefined it to mean a religious activity, a prayer, (page 424 of the opinion) to have public school children hear or recite a prayer that "somebody in government composed" (pages 425-427 of the opinion). "...writing or sanctioning official prayers" (page 435 of the opinion) and government "endorsement" of a prayer (page 436 of the opinion).

These six judges, Black, Warren, Clark, Harlan, Brennan, and Douglas also admitted that even though no coercion was present, and even though the prayer was denomination neutral, it still constituted an unlawful establishment of religion.

The majority opinion, written by Judge Black, continues on page 430:

> "The Establishment Clause" of the First Amendment "does not depend upon any showing of direct governmental compulsion and is violated by the enactment of laws which establish an official religion whether those laws operate directly to coerce non-observing individuals or not."

Douglas said on pages 438 and 439 in his concurring opinion:

> "There is no element of compulsion or coercion in New York's regulation requiring that public schools be opened each day with the...prayer." "...there is...no effort at indoctrination, and no attempt at exposition...New York's prayer...does not involve any element of proselytizing."

Established religion was redefined to describe what the New York public schools were doing. Only then could it be outlawed.

The judges admitted on page 436 of the majority opinion that allowing school children to say this prayer did not really establish a religion and that the prayer:

> "...does not amount to a total establishment of one particular religious sect to the exclusion of all others; that, indeed, the governmental endorsement of that prayer seems relatively insignificant when compared to the governmental encroachments upon religion which were commonplace 200 years ago."

Douglas wrote in his concurring opinion (Page 442):

> "I cannot say that to authorize this prayer is to establish
> a religion in the strictly historic meaning of those words.
> A religion is not established in the usual sense merely by
> letting those who choose to do so say the prayer that the
> public school teacher leads."

Since the Supreme Court in Engel v. Vitale says it sought to protect our
public school children from reciting or hearing, if they wanted to, a one-
sentence non-denominational prayer which somebody in government
composed, it would make sense that dilemma could be avoided if the
children write their own prayers. But six judges on the Supreme Court
in Santa Fe Independent School Dist. v. Doe (2000) said "no" to that
option.

Here a public school district permitted, but did not require, student-
initiated, student-led, nonsectarian, non-proselytizing prayer at home
football games.

But Justices Stevens, Ginsberg, Souter, Breyer, O'Connor, and Kennedy
said this constituted an "establishment" of religion in violation of
the First Amendment, because the prayers were "public speech"
authorized by "government policy," taking place on "government
property" at government sponsored school events, and the policy
involved perceived an actual "government endorsement of prayer."

They cite themselves as authority on page 310 of the opinion:

> "We explained in *Lee* that the 'preservation and
> transmission of religious beliefs and worship is a
> responsibility and a choice committed to the private
> sphere."

However, the Constitution does not restrict religion to the private
sphere. It forbids Congress from prohibiting its free exercise anywhere.

Again, the six judges in Santa Fe redefined establishment of religion to
describe what the Santa Fe School District was doing. By doing so, they
could rule on it.

On page 318 of his dissenting opinion, Rehnquist, joined by Scalia and Thomas, said the majority opinion "bristles with hostility to all things religious in public life. Neither the holding nor the tone of the opinion is faithful to the meaning of the Establishment Clause, when it is recalled that George Washington himself, at the request of the very Congress which passed the Bill of Rights, proclaimed a day of public thanksgiving and prayer, to be observed by acknowledging with grateful hearts the many and signal favors of Almighty God."

The Wall of Separation Between Church and State

The phrase "wall of separation between church and state" is nowhere in the Constitution, and it is not a constitutional principle.

The First Amendment says Congress may not lawfully establish one religious creed as official truth and support it with its full financial and coercive powers and it may not prohibit the free exercise of religion or religious speech anywhere.

Below is the origin of the phrase in question:

We saw earlier in Connecticut that the Congregational Church was the established religion until Connecticut abolished that church with its Constitution of 1818. Earlier, on October 7, 1801, Baptists in Danbury, Connecticut wrote a letter to President Thomas Jefferson in which they expressed their distress that they were a religious minority in Connecticut. They said:

> "...religion is considered as the first object of legislation; and therefore what religious privileges we enjoy (as a minor part of the State) we enjoy as favors granted, and not as inalienable rights; and these favors we receive at the expense of such degrading acknowledgments as are inconsistent with the rights of freemen. Sir, we are sensible that the president of the United States is not the national legislator, and also sensible that the national government cannot destroy the laws of each State; but our hopes are strong that the sentiments of our beloved president, which have had such genial effect already, like the radiant beams of the sun, will shine and prevail through all these States...till...tyranny be destroyed from the earth."

The Baptists expressed their hope that the people of Connecticut would be influenced by Jefferson's sentiments and abolish the Congregational Church in Connecticut.

In his response dated January 2, 1802, Jefferson indicated that he hoped that the people of Connecticut would follow the example of the whole American people:

> "Believing with you that religion is a matter which lies solely between man and his God, that he owes account to none other for his faith or his worship, that the legitimate powers of government reach actions only, and not opinions, I contemplate with sovereign reverence that act of the whole American people which declared that their legislature should make no law respecting an establishment of religion, or prohibiting the free exercise thereof, thus building a wall of separation between Church and State. Adhering to this expression of the supreme will of the nation in behalf of the rights of conscience, I shall see with sincere satisfaction the progress of those sentiments which tend to restore to man all his natural rights."

Jefferson agreed that civil government ought not dictate to citizens in matters of religious belief, and pointed out that the First Amendment prevents Congress from doing this. He did not say religion must be relegated to the private sphere. He used the First Amendment as his model to affirm that it restricts only Congress, not religion.

In the case above, Engel v. Vitale, Hugo Black said on page 425 of the majority opinion that the reading of the prayer breaches the constitutional wall of separation between church and state.

Even though this metaphor of "wall of separation between church and State" is nowhere in the Constitution, this Supreme Court judge misrepresented it as a constitutional principle.

In summary, the Supreme Court, not the people, has violated the First Amendment with regards to free speech and free exercise of religion in four ways:

1. Even though the First Amendment expressly restricts only Congress, and thus was intended to be the states' and the peoples' protection from Congress, the Supreme Court reversed the purpose of the First Amendment so it became the tool which the court uses to suppress the free exercise of a religion throughout the states, counties, towns, and villages, all the way down to football fields and county courthouse lawns.

2. Even though the authors of the First Amendment defined an establishment of religion in a historical context, the federal courts from time to time have redefined the term. As a result, the Supreme Court can declare circumstances surrounding religious speech as unconstitutional, thus amending the U.S. Constitution through court opinions.

3. They outlawed the free exercise of religion, and they outlawed free speech when the subject was religious. The courts took away from their creators a right reserved in the U.S. Constitution. Neither the Supreme Court nor Congress may stop people from praying anywhere, or stop people from posting the Ten Commandments anywhere, or stop people from preaching in any public areas. In fact, all three branches of the federal government are prohibited from even addressing the subject of religion for the nation as a whole since religion is not an enumerated power.

4. When Congress is prohibited from making laws in an area, the Supreme Court may not make laws in that area. The only way a religion or speech issue could ever be argued before the Supreme Court would be if Congress violated the First Amendment and Article I, Section 8, by creating a law respecting the establishment of religion or prohibiting the free exercise thereof, or by making a law abridging the freedom of speech.

The United States and political subdivisions retain the rights to make whatever laws they please in respect to religion, subject only to any limitations imposed by their own state constitutions. The U.S. Supreme Court has no constitutional authority whatsoever to interfere in that law creating process. By claiming their opinions have the effect of law, they have made laws in respect to religion, and laws to abridge speech, even though the federal government does not have any authority to act in this area.

Related Questions and Research Assignments

1. Paraphrase the following segment of James Madison's Federalist Paper No. 42:

"The defect of power in the existing Confederacy to regulate the commerce between its several members, is in the number of those which have been clearly pointed out by experience. To the proofs and remarks which former papers have brought into view on this subject, it may be added that without this supplemental provision, the great and essential power of regulating foreign commerce would have been incomplete and ineffectual. A very material object of this power was the relief of the States which import and export through other States, from the improper contributions levied on them by the latter. Were these at liberty to regulate the trade between State and State, it must be foreseen that ways would be found out to load the articles of import and export, during the passage through their jurisdiction, with duties which would fall on the makers of the latter and the consumers of the former. We may be assured by past experience, that such a practice would be introduced by future contrivances; and both by that and a common knowledge of human affairs, that it would nourish unceasing animosities, and not improbably terminate in serious interruptions of the public tranquillity. To those who do not view the question through the medium of passion or of interest, the desire of the commercial States to collect, in any form, an indirect revenue from their uncommercial neighbors, must appear not less impolitic than it is unfair; since it would stimulate the injured party, by resentment as well as interest, to resort to less convenient channels for their foreign trade. But the mild voice of reason, pleading the cause of an enlarged and permanent interest, is but too often drowned,

before public bodies as well as individuals, by the clamors
of an impatient avidity for immediate and immoderate gain."

2. Paraphrase the following segment of Alexander Hamilton's
Federalist Paper No. 32:

"An entire consolidation of the States into one complete
national sovereignty would imply an entire subordination
of the parts; and whatever powers might remain in them,
would be altogether dependent on the general will. But
as the plan of the convention aims only at a partial union
or consolidation, the State governments would clearly
retain all the rights of sovereignty which they before
had, and which were not, by that act, EXCLUSIVELY
delegated to the United States. This exclusive delegation,
or rather this alienation, of State sovereignty, would only
exist in three cases: where the Constitution in express
terms granted an exclusive authority to the Union; where
it granted in one instance an authority to the Union,
and in another prohibited the States from exercising
the like authority; and where it granted an authority
to the Union, to which a similar authority in the States
would be absolutely and totally CONTRADICTORY
and REPUGNANT. I use these terms to distinguish this
last case from another which might appear to resemble
it, but which would, in fact, be essentially different; I
mean where the exercise of a concurrent jurisdiction
might be productive of occasional interferences in the
POLICY of any branch of administration, but would not
imply any direct contradiction or repugnancy in point of
constitutional authority. These three cases of exclusive
jurisdiction in the federal government may be exemplified
by the following instances: The last clause but one in the
eighth section of the first article provides expressly that
Congress shall exercise "EXCLUSIVE LEGISLATION"
over the district to be appropriated as the seat of
government. This answers to the first case. The first clause
of the same section empowers Congress "TO LAY AND

COLLECT TAXES, DUTIES, IMPOSTS AND EXCISES"; and the second clause of the tenth section of the same article declares that, "NO STATE SHALL, without the consent of Congress, LAY ANY IMPOSTS OR DUTIES ON IMPORTS OR EXPORTS, except for the purpose of executing its inspection laws." Hence would result an exclusive power in the Union to lay duties on imports and exports, with the particular exception mentioned; but this power is abridged by another clause, which declares that no tax or duty shall be laid on articles exported from any State; in consequence of which qualification, it now only extends to the DUTIES ON IMPORTS. This answers to the second case. The third will be found in that clause which declares that Congress shall have power 'to establish an UNIFORM RULE of naturalization throughout the United States.' This must necessarily be exclusive; because if each State had power to prescribe a DISTINCT RULE, there could not be a UNIFORM RULE."

3. Research the complaint presented in the 1925 case of Gitlow v. People. How did the Supreme Court justices justify their opinions?

4. Based on history, explain the differences between a tolerated religion and an established religion.

5. In your own words, restate the First Amendment. To whom does it apply?

6. From where did the phrase "separation of church and State" come?

   a. What was the circumstance of the letter from which this phrase was taken, and what was the original intent of its usage?
   b. When was the phrase first used in a Supreme Court opinion and how was it not applied correctly?

7. Use a highlighter, color of your choice, to highlight four references to God in our Declaration of Independence.

Chapter 8

AMENDMENTS

Consider the logic of the following statements:

- If your spouse violates the marriage vows, amend the vows and your marriage will be saved.
- If motorists violate the speed limit, amend the speed limit and safety will be restored.
- When people violate the Ten Commandments, amend the Ten Commandments and morality will prevail.

When politicians at the federal level violate their oath and the Constitution by (1) spending what is not authorized, or (2) making laws on subjects with no authorization, many citizens and legislators advocate amendments to the U.S. Constitution to resolve the issue.

Is the Constitution the problem or is this a personal integrity problem?

How will amendments to the Constitution cure shortcomings of personal integrity?

When the Constitution is not the problem, why change it?

The framers acknowledged in the Federalist Papers that the novelty and difficulty of what they were doing would require periodic revision. They did not see the purpose of amendments as the way to control the federal government. It was to remedy *defects* in the Constitution itself. Hamilton said in Federalist Paper No. 85 that useful amendments would address the organization of the government, not the "mass of its powers."

Madison said in Federalist Paper No. 43 that "useful alterations will be suggested by experience."

The 12th Amendment, ratified in 1804, was one suggested by experience. It fixed an irregularity in the process of electing the President. At the election of 1800, the electors gave John Adams the highest number of votes while Jefferson was given the second highest number. So Adams became President and Jefferson became Vice President. But Adams and Jefferson were political opponents. The 12th Amendment was designed to fix that. As a result, the electors could ensure that they voted for compatible people when they cast their vote for President and Vice President.

The 13th Amendment, ratified in 1865, recognized the defect of slavery that the Constitution did not.

The 11th Amendment, ratified 1795, reduced the powers of the federal courts by reducing their jurisdiction. It prohibits them from hearing cases filed against a state by citizens of another state, or by citizens or subjects of any foreign country.

Generally speaking, amendments at the federal level can have unintended or unfortunate outcomes because:

- Amendments generally do not stand alone as they are subject to opinions of the federal courts.
- Most amendments do not amend the real problem.
- The amendment record so far has not followed the founders' intention.
- Results of an amendment can be different than expected by the citizens.

1. Amendments generally do not stand alone as they are subject to opinions of the federal courts. This is an overlooked aspect of amending the Constitution.

    Article III, Section 2, clause 1, states:

"The judicial Power shall extend to all Cases, in Law
and Equity, arising under this Constitution..."

The important thing to remember is that once the amendment
is ratified, the subject of that amendment now arises under the
Constitution and is vulnerable to the opinions of the federal
courts. The passage of an amendment is just the beginning
and it may be generations before the full effects, detrimental or
otherwise, will be felt.

Who could have foreseen that the passage of the First
Amendment would result in court opinions which would
ban prayer in schools, crosses on hills, or Bible display in
courthouses? But it did.

Hamilton foresaw such a conclusion. He warned in Federalist
Paper No. 84, 9th paragraph, that amendments would give a
pretext for regulating our rights to those inclined to usurp powers.

> "I go further, and affirm that bills of rights, in the
> sense and to the extent in which they are contended
> for, are not only unnecessary in the proposed
> Constitution, but would even be dangerous. They
> would contain various exceptions to powers not
> granted; and, on this very account, would afford a
> colorable pretext to claim more than were granted.
> For why declare that things shall not be done
> which there is no power to do? Why, for instance,
> should it be said that the liberty of the press shall
> not be restrained, when no power is given by which
> restrictions may be imposed? I will not contend that
> such a provision would confer a regulating power; but
> it is evident that it would furnish, to men disposed to
> usurp, a plausible pretense for claiming that power."

Who could have foreseen the loss of state sovereignty with the
passage of the 17th Amendment when state sovereignty was not
even the subject of the amendment?

Who could have foreseen the loss of personal freedoms with the passage of the 16th Amendment which gives Congress access to our personal income?

Who could have foreseen federal court opinions that would link the 14th Amendment with the First Amendment, resulting in the loss of state powers over matters the framers specifically provided to the states?

2. Most amendments do not attack the real problem.

The real problem is one of personal virtue and integrity in our elected officials. Violating a promise, or an oath, is a moral problem, not a legislative one. Every elected official at the federal and state level took an oath to support the Constitution, not to violate it. Spending and other problems created by Congress are directly related to elected representatives who act outside the boundaries they agreed to when they took office with no permission to do so.

This is not a problem with a deficient document. According to the founders, the remedy for this is the election of more virtuous and knowledgeable representatives, not changing the Constitution.

3. The amendment record so far has not followed the founders' intentions.

Some citizens, legislators, and activists insist the only way to correct a federal government which violates the intent and rules in the constitution is amendments.

To date, there have been twenty-seven amendments to our Constitution.

Of the fifteen amendments ratified since the 12th in 1804, ten increased the powers of the federal government: 13th, 14th, 15th, 16th, 17th, 18th, 19th, 23rd, 24th, and the 26th. Four were housekeeping amendments that further clarified minor election and legislative procedures: 20th, 22nd, 25th, and the 27th.

Five of the first ten amendments are not even amendments—1st, 2nd, 3rd, 9th, and 10th—as they amend nothing. If they were not there, meaning of the constitution would be exactly the same. Those amendments simply affirmed natural rights that already existed. The rest of the ten are simply a list of things the federal government cannot do, like take away people's guns, and a list of some things they must do, like insuring fair trials.

4. Here are examples of how the results of an amendment can be different than how it was presented to the citizens.

    A. On February 13, 2013, U.S. Senator John Cornyn offered an amendment which intended to balance the budget. This amendment was presented to the public by the Senator, his co-sponsors, and the media as a restriction on Congress's spending. Here are the first two points of the amendment.

    Section 1. "Total outlays for any fiscal year shall not exceed total receipts for that fiscal year, unless two-thirds of the duly chosen and sworn Members of each House of Congress shall provide by law for a specific excess of outlays over receipts by a roll call vote."

    Does this mean that we will spend only what we take in as it was presented? Can it also mean that the more we take in, the more we can spend? That is still balanced.

    Can it possibly mean that we will not spend any more than we take in unless we vote to spend more than we take in?

    Section 2. "Total outlays for any fiscal year shall not exceed 18 percent of the gross domestic product of the United States for the calendar year ending before the beginning of such fiscal year, unless two-thirds of the duly chosen and sworn Members of each House of Congress shall provide by law for a specific amount in excess of such 18 percent by a roll call vote."

Is this granting Congress permission to spend up to 18 percent of the GDP, whether they need it or not? Or might it mean that they will not spend more than 18 percent of the GDP unless they vote to spend more than 18 percent of the GDP? Where in the Constitution is the permission to link spending to production, output, inflation, population change, or any subject whatsoever other than the enumerated objects previously discussed? This might be construed as a new permission to spend, not a restriction as it was presented.

B. The below proposed amendment was presented as one that was designed to "limit the federal bureaucracy."[1]

> "All federal departments and agencies shall expire if said departments and agencies are not individually reauthorized in stand-alone reauthorization bills every three years by a majority vote of the House of Representatives and the Senate."

According to this wording, as long as Congress periodically reauthorizes the agencies, they remain.

How does that limit the bureaucracy? In addition, this amendment changes the constitutional standard for an existing executive agency from whether it carries out an enumerated power, as in Washington's cabinet, to whatever the president wants and to which Congress agrees.

---

[1]   Page 99-100, *The Liberty Amendments* by Mark Levin

George Washington's cabinet had six members: Vice President, Secretary of State, Secretary of War, Secretary of the Treasury, and Attorney General, and Postmaster General. Those functions are authorized by our Constitution.

Today there are numerous agencies in the Executive Branch of the federal government with no constitutional authority to even exist. What Article, Section, and clause authorizes the Departments of Agriculture, Education, Energy, Labor, Transportation, HHS, HUD, DHS, EPA, SBA, etc.?

There is no constitutional authority.

Therefore, all of these agencies are unconstitutional since they practice outside the scope of the powers delegated in our Constitution. This amendment would legalize these agencies.

C. Another section of the same proposed amendment presented for the purpose of limiting the bureaucracy:

> "All Executive Branch regulations exceeding an economic burden of $100 million, as determined jointly by the Government Accountability Office and the Congressional Budget Office, shall be submitted to a permanent Joint Committee of Congress, hereafter the Congressional Delegation Oversight Committee, for review and approval prior to their implementation."

This amendment legalizes all Executive Branch regulations and the rule making process of a certain amount, but as we have seen earlier, only Congress may make laws. How does this "limit the bureaucracy?" This proposed amendment does the opposite of what it proposes.

D. This one was presented for the purpose of limiting federal spending from the same book.

> "Congress shall adopt a preliminary fiscal year budget no later than the first Monday in May for the following fiscal year, and submit said budget to the President for consideration."[2]

Our Constitution limits federal spending to the enumerated powers. That is how our framers controlled federal spending. It is the enumerated powers which limit spending, not the amount of revenue the federal government generates or the size of the GDP, inflation, or any other reason.

This amendment legalizes all the spending which is now unconstitutional. It legalizes the budget process whereby the President and Congress adopt a budget and spend money on whatever they put in the budget.

---

[2] Page 73- 74, *The Liberty Amendments* by Mark Levin

Article V Convention

The federal convention of 1787 was called by the Continental Congress for the sole and express purpose of revising the Articles of Confederation. The process they used should serve as a warning about such a convention to amend the Constitution in the future.

The delegates to the 1787 convention:

- Ignored their instructions from the Continental Congress and from their states.
- Ignored Article XIII of the Articles of Confederation which required the states to obey Congress on matters covered by the Articles.
- Wrote an entirely new Constitution with a new method of ratification which required only nine of the thirteen states for ratification because once the convention started, the delegates made no rules which prevented the change in ratification procedures.

The deficiencies of amendments to correct government mischief have been documented in previous chapters and in this chapter above. Therefore, no logical argument can be made for that effort.

The framers never suggested that the purpose of amendments was to correct behavioral problems of elected officials. The states and the people were expected by our framers to do that through elections, education, and nullification.

Our framers did not consider these conventions a wise move. Mr. Pinckney, as recorded on page 632 of the Records of the Federal Convention on September 15, 1787 said,

> "Conventions are serious things, and ought not to be repeated."

Alexander Hamilton in Federalist Paper No. 85, 9th paragraph, wrote:

> "the utter improbability of assembling a new convention, under circumstances in any degree so favorable to a happy issue, as those in which the late convention met, deliberated, and concluded."

James Madison said to Turberville in his letter of November 2, 1788:

> "If a General Convention were to take place for the avowed and sole purpose of revising the Constitution, it would naturally consider itself as having a greater latitude than the Congress appointed to administer and support as well as to amend the system; it would consequently give greater agitation to the public mind; an election into it would be courted by the most violent partizans on both sides; it wd. probably consist of the most heterogeneous characters; would be the very focus of that flame which has already too much heated men of all parties; would no doubt contain individuals of insidious views, who under the mask of seeking alterations popular in some parts but inadmissible in other parts of the Union might have a dangerous opportunity of sapping the very foundations of the fabric. Under all these circumstances it seems scarcely to be presumeable that the deliberations of the body could be conducted in harmony, or terminate in the general good."

Farther down in the same letter, Madison commented:

> "Having witnessed the difficulties and dangers experienced by the first Convention which assembled under every propitious circumstance, I should tremble for the result of a Second meeting in the present temper of America and under all the disadvantages I have mentioned."

Article V advocates ignore our founders' advice, proposing using an Article V convention to propose amendments anyway.

Here is the applicable part of Article V as written in the Constitution:

> "The Congress, whenever two thirds of both Houses shall deem it necessary, shall propose Amendments to this Constitution, or, on the Application of the Legislatures of two thirds of the several States, shall call a Convention for proposing Amendments, which, in either Case, shall be valid to all Intents and Purposes, as part of this Constitution, when ratified by the Legislatures of three fourths of the several States, or by Conventions in three fourths thereof, as the one or the other Mode of Ratification may be proposed by the Congress;"

Article V, as illustrated above, provides two methods of proposing amendments to the Constitution. Congress either (1) "shall propose" the amendments, or (2) Congress "shall call" a convention when the legislatures of two thirds of the states apply for it. A proper reading shows that Congress alone has the responsibility for any convention. States may only "make application."

The first method is the one that has been used for all twenty-seven amendments we have now, including the Bill of Rights which were introduced into Congress by James Madison.

The second method has gone by several titles in the past. It has been called a constitutional convention, a con-con, an Article V convention, or most recently, a convention of States. The term, "convention of States," is deceptive as only Congress, not the states, has the power to call it. Since Article I, Section 8, last clause, vests in Congress all powers "necessary and proper" to carry out its power, then *calling* a convention falls under that clause. Congress, not the states, may decide all organizational issues, such as, the number and selection process for delegates under the authority of the necessary and proper clause.

But once the delegates are seated, neither Congress nor the states have any control over them. The delegates can do whatever they want. They can even propose a new Constitution if they choose and no one can stop them.

The second point to consider is that the U.S. Congress has financial leverage over the states since the states are dependent on federal funding to balance their own budgets. Reid Wilson writes in his September 23, 2013 article in the Washington Post that,

> "Federal grants accounted for more than one-third of State budget revenues in fiscal year 2011, according to data compiled by the Pew Charitable Trusts Fiscal Federalism Initiative."

If these Article V advocates depend on the states to make demands on the federal government, will the federal government, in turn, threaten to withhold funds the states need to balance their own budgets? Will the states risk losing federal funds on which they now depend for such matters as education, transportation, housing, national parks, and so forth?

A third point to consider is the rules the states themselves set up for the delegates. In the past, to set up rules for the states delegates, state legislators introduced legislation that limited what their delegates could or could not do since Article V in the Constitution does not say. Even if one state's delegates was to remain within the boundaries set by the state legislature, what is to bind the delegates from the other forty-nine states, and prevent them from overstepping the people's wishes? What if one state is in favor of abolishing our present Constitution and convinces others to join it?

In summation, if a constitutional convention was requested by the required number of states for the sole purpose of amendments, the chances of a good outcome may not be favorable. We must consider:

- Amendments generally do not stand alone as they are subject to opinions of the federal courts.
- Most amendments do not amend the real problem.
- The amendment record so far has not followed the founders' intent.
- Results of an amendment can be different than expected by the citizens.

The National Popular Vote versus the 12th and the17th Amendments

History has shown that the Constitution has been opposed by one faction or another since the day of ratification. One of the most pernicious of attacks is by those who seek to override the constitutional provisions under which the states, as political entities, elect the president, and to replace it with a national popular vote (NPV) under which inhabitants of major metropolitan areas will have an advantage to choose the president, which disregards the votes of the rural communities.

In order for the states to maintain their independence and sovereignty, our framers wrote these provisions into our Constitution:

- The states, as separate political entities, were to elect the President and Vice President, Article II, Section 1, clauses 2-3.
- The state legislatures were to choose the two U.S. Senators for their State, Article I, Section 3, clause 1.

Our framers, after considering their extensive study of history, never intended for the president, vice president, or members to the senate to be elected by a national popular vote as they are today, but by the state legislatures.

The people were to elect the members of the House as their representatives. That was the part of Congress whose allegiance would be only to the people.

James Madison, Father of Our Constitution, explains in Federalist Paper No. 45, 3rd paragraph, why this ensured that the states would maintain control over the national government.

> "The State governments may be regarded as constituent and
> essential parts of the federal government; whilst the latter
> is nowise essential to the operation or organization of the
> former. Without the intervention of the State legislatures, the

President of the United States cannot be elected at all. They must in all cases have a great share in his appointment, and will, perhaps, in most cases, of themselves determine it. The Senate will be elected absolutely and exclusively by the State legislatures. Even the House of Representatives, though drawn immediately from the people, will be chosen very much under the influence of that class of men, whose influence over the people obtains for themselves an election into the State legislatures. Thus each of the principal branches of the federal government will owe its existence more or less to the favor of the State governments, and must consequently feel a dependence, which is much more likely to beget a disposition too obsequious than too overbearing towards them."

In Federalist Paper No. 62, it was explained that the appointment of senators by state legislatures was to secure the authority of the state governments in the federal government, and to preserve the sovereignty remaining in the individual states.

Federalist No. 62, 7th paragraph, shows another advantage of the state legislatures' appointments of U.S. Senators:

"Another advantage accruing from this ingredient in the constitution of the Senate is, the additional impediment it must prove against improper acts of legislation. No law or resolution can now be passed without the concurrence, first, of a majority of the people, and then, of a majority of the States."

Since representatives to the House were chosen by popular vote of the people, and U.S. Senators were to be chosen by the state legislatures, no law could get passed by Congress unless it was approved by the people—via their representatives and by the states via the appointed U.S. Senators.

This is what our framers gave us to protect us from a Congress bent on usurpations of their delegated authority.

In Federalist Paper No. 64, John Jay explained that the electors would be "select assemblies" "composed of the most enlightened and respectable citizens" who would vote for those men who were "the most distinguished by their abilities and virtue." Furthermore, electors would not likely "be deceived by those brilliant appearances of genius and patriotism" which "sometimes mislead as well as dazzle."

In all of Federalist 68, Hamilton elaborated on the same idea and explains the wisdom of specially selected electors who were "most likely to possess information and discernment" elect the president.

He also warns,

> "These most deadly adversaries of republican government might naturally have been expected to make their approaches from more than one quarter, but chiefly from the desire in foreign powers to gain an improper ascendant in our councils. How could they better gratify this, than by raising a creature of their own to the chief magistracy of the Union?"

Now that we see why our framers provided that electors from the member states were to choose the president of the federation, let us see how the voting is to be conducted.

The long ignored, but never repealed, 12th Amendment, ratified in 1804, sets forth binding procedures for taking and counting the electors' votes.

The electors in each state are to meet and cast their votes for president and vice president separately. Assume a state has 13 electors and the voting goes like this:

For President:

Mr. Falconer–6 votes
Mr. Lossie–5 votes
Mr. Bell–2 votes

For Vice President:

Mr. Cross–5 votes
Mr. Duncan–5 votes
Mr. Nichols–3 votes.

The electors sign and certify this list and send it to the President of the Senate. On the appointed day, and in front of a joint session of Congress, the President of the Senate counts the electors' votes from the member states.

The person with the greatest number of votes for president becomes the president if he has a majority. The person with the greatest number of votes for vice president becomes the vice president if he has a majority. If one or both do not have a majority, the rest is explained in the amendment.

Prior to the 17th Amendment, this is how our Constitution required the elections of president and vice president to be conducted.

The states, as political entities and as the members of the federation, are the ones who were to choose the president, vice president, and senators. This is what our framers gave us to protect us from a Congress bent on mischief against the states. It also gave the smaller states a voice in the selection of president.

The result of the state legislatures (1) choosing the U.S. Senators and (2) controlling the election of the president and vice president, is that the states would control the national government and keep it in line.

With the 17th Amendment in 1913, the election of members of the U.S. Senate was now in the hands of the citizens, rather than the state legislatures. This is how the states, the members of the federation, lost their representation in Congress and their control over that body. U.S. Senators no longer needed to answer to the wishes of their own states.

As time went on, the national political system chose to disregard the framers' intent of the election of the president by the states when a new system was accepted whereby national political parties handle the elections of president and vice president. Instead of the small bodies of specially chosen wise and prudent men who actually made the selections, electors became obligated for the popular vote in their states.

Instead of the electors choosing the vice president, now the party bosses, then party nominees, choose the running mates. Instead of the electors' votes transmitted to the President of the Senate with the total votes listed for each person who receives votes, states awarded all their electoral votes to the person who won the popular vote in their state.

This is how the states, the members of the federation, lost their control over the election of the president.

To further dilute the voting system, there are some that are calling for the national popular election of the president as well.

What is the answer in order to return to the founders' intent?

- Elect to Congress only those who are committed to repealing the 17th Amendment. This is the only way the states can regain control of Congress.
- Return to the 12th Amendment. We must dismantle the present unconstitutional system and return to the method of electing the president and vice president established in our Constitution. State legislators could immediately restore to their states the power to control the election of the president. All states have to obey the 12th Amendment. Also, specially chosen electors are far more likely to choose good presidents than the many citizen voters who have not made a study of history or of our Constitution.

As a result, costly state primaries or national conventions would not be needed. Expensive advertising which excludes the candidates who are not wealthy would be eliminated. Voting machines could be eliminated. Congress could repeal unconstitutional federal laws which restrict political speech. There would be no need for candidates to promise future favors in return for campaign contributions. U.S. Senators would not be so inclined to vote for legislation that would cost the state citizens' tax money such as Medicaid does today. In short, the temptation of corruption which permeates our present system would be reduced.

Even in its present unconstitutional form, the Electoral College serves two important purposes. It balances the influence of the heavily populated urban areas, which typically vote one way with the sparsely populated rural areas that typically vote the other way. It gives the smaller states a voice in the election of president.

Here is a bit of wisdom from Thomas Jefferson's letter of February 2, 1816 to Joseph C. Cabell:

> "...the way to have good and safe government, is not to trust it all to one, but to divide it among the many, distributing to every one exactly the functions he is competent to. Let the national government be entrusted with the defence of the nation, and its foreign and federal relations; the State governments with the civil rights, laws, police, and administration of what concerns the State generally; the counties with the local concerns of the counties, and each ward direct the interests within itself. It is by dividing and subdividing these republics from the great national one down through all its subordinations, until it ends in the administration of every man's farm by himself; by placing under every one what his own eye may superintend, that all will be done for the best. What has destroyed liberty and the rights of man in every government which has ever existed under the sun? The generalizing and concentrating all cares and power into one body."

The 14th Amendment and Same-sex Marriage

Does the 14th Amendment require a state to license a marriage of two people of the same sex?

Does the 14th Amendment require a state to recognize a marriage of two people of the same sex when their marriage was lawfully licensed and performed out of state?

These were the two questions presented for the Supreme Court to decide during April 2015 oral arguments in *Obergefell v Hodges* and consolidated cases.

Section 1 of the 14th Amendment says:

> "All persons born or naturalized in the United States, and subject to the jurisdiction thereof, are citizens of the United States and of the State wherein they reside. No State shall make or enforce any law which shall abridge the privileges or immunities of citizens of the United States; nor shall any State deprive any person of life, liberty, or property, without due process of law; nor deny to any person within its jurisdiction the equal protection of the law."

Section 1 says nothing about marriage or homosexuality. How can it authorize the Supreme Court to force states to accept same sex marriage?

What the court had to do in order to be able to accept the case was to redefine liberty in Section 1 so it meant privacy. Now that privacy has been determined to be a constitutional right, as in Roe v. Wade, "privacy" now "arises" under the Constitution and, in the Court's eyes, falls under their jurisdiction to hear and issue an opinion on the case.

Privacy is a natural right, not a constitutional right. But the Court said under Part VIII of their opinion:

> "This right of privacy, whether it be founded in the Fourteenth Amendment's concept of personal liberty and restrictions upon State action, as we feel it is broad enough to encompass a woman's decision whether or not to terminate her pregnancy."

In Lawrence v. Texas in 2003, the court looked at the word, "liberty" in Section 1 and said that it means consenting adults have the right to engage in private acts of homosexuality. Since the federal judges have decided that they can rule on such subjects, the opinion could have gone the other way, making homosexuality illegal. They determined in that paragraph,

> "We conclude the case should be resolved by determining whether the petitioners were free as adults to engage in the private conduct in the exercise of their liberty under the Due Process Clause of the Fourteenth Amendment."

And in the third paragraph from the end, they declare,

> "The case does involve two adults who, with full and mutual consent from each other, engaged in sexual practices common to a homosexual lifestyle. The petitioners are entitled to respect for their private lives. The state cannot demean their existence or control their destiny by making their private sexual conduct a crime. Their right to liberty under the Due Process Clause gives them the full right to engage in their conduct…"

The Supreme Court uses the word "liberty" in Section 1 of the 14th Amendment to justify which behavioral practices the court may decide. By claiming that these practices constitute liberty rights which arise under Section 1 of the 14th Amendment, they evade the constitutional limits on their judicial power.

Hamilton does not agree.

Alexander Hamilton writes in Federalist Paper No. 83, 8th paragraph:

> "In like manner the judicial authority of the federal judicatures is declared by the Constitution to comprehend certain cases particularly specified. The expression of those cases marks the precise limits, beyond which the federal courts cannot extend their jurisdiction, because the objects of their cognizance being enumerated, the specification would be nugatory if it did not exclude all ideas of more extensive authority."

In Federalist Paper No. 80, Hamilton explains the categories of cases over which federal courts have jurisdiction. If a case does not fit within one of these categories, federal courts may not hear it.

Since the right to same sex marriage is claimed by the court to arise under Section 1 of the 14th Amendment, we will focus on Hamilton's discussion of cases "arising under this Constitution" or as Hamilton puts it, cases "...which concern the execution of the provisions expressly contained in the articles of Union..."

Hamilton then gives examples of such "expressly contained" cases. Article I, Section 10, prohibit states from imposing duties on imported articles, or from issuing paper money. In those cases, the federal courts are in the best position to overrule infractions which are contrary to the Constitution.

Where are provisions which address marriage and homosexuality "expressly contained" in our Constitution?

Power to regulate the subject of abortion, homosexuality, and marriage is not delegated to the national government for the country as a whole by our Constitution.

The Supreme Court has usurped power over these objects. Their opinions are void for lack of jurisdiction and are proper objects of nullification.

Shari´a Law versus the First Amendment

Shari´a Law advocates claim to have a First Amendment right to build mosques, proselytize, and implement Shari´a Law here. But is that what the First Amendment says? It says:

> "Congress shall make no law respecting an establishment of religion, or prohibiting the free exercise thereof; or abridging the freedom of speech, or of the press; or the right of the people peaceably to assemble, and to petition the Government for a redress of grievances."

The First Amendment does not grant any rights to anyone. All it does is to prohibit Congress from making laws respecting the subjects of religion, speech, the press, or assembly.

And recall, in the much larger issue, Article VI, clause 2, of our Constitution says:

> "This Constitution, and the Laws of the United States which shall be made in Pursuance thereof; and all Treaties made, or which shall be made, under the Authority of the United States, shall be the supreme Law of the Land; and the Judges in every State shall be bound thereby, any Thing in the Constitution or Laws of any State to the Contrary notwithstanding."

Our Constitution only recognizes those laws which were made by the representatives the citizens voted into office as the law of the land.

Those laws, if made pursuant to the Constitution, protect the natural rights God gave each person. One of those natural rights is to worship as we please. Shari´a law is contrary to the free exercise of worship.

Let's look at just one God-given right: the right to a fair trial.

- Bearing false witness is condemned by the Ten Commandments.
- The evidence of two or more witnesses is required to prove a case as explained in Deuteronomy 19:15 and Matthew 18:16.
- Public trials are required as shown in Exodus 18:13.
- Judges are required to be fair, impartial, without favoritism as explained in Deuteronomy 1:16-17.

In Iran, judges using Shari´a Law in "morals" cases, such as adultery, are allowed to make their own subjective determinations that a person is guilty even in the absence of any evidence.

Shari´a Law makes no distinction between religious and political spheres of government. The Constitution, on the other hand, restricts the federal government's intrusion into citizen's personal lives.

Our Constitution and laws which are authorized by the Constitution are the supreme law of the land. Anything to the contrary must fall. It violates the Constitution to practice Shari´a in the United States. Those who seek to replace our Constitution and the laws under its authority with Shari´a are guilty of criminal sedition. All members of the federal government took the oath to support the Constitution and have the duty to prosecute them for sedition, or deport them.

Parental Rights Amendment

The Parental Rights Amendment (PRA) strips parents of their God-delegated authority over their children, transferring that authority to the federal government, despite the name of the amendment.

The subject of children is one which is reserved in the Constitution to be addressed by the states or the people. It is not a lawful subject which the federal government may address, either by legislation or treaty, unless there is an amendment that changes that.

Enter the Parental Rights Amendment (PRA) which was introduced into Congress in June of 2013 as H. J. Res. 50.

Amendments are part of the Constitution. Therefore federal courts have power to decide issues addressed by amendments. The PRA would transform families and children from matters over which the federal government now has no lawful authority to matters under the total control of the federal government should such an amendment be ratified.

Here are some relevant parts of the amendment as introduced.

> "Section 1: The liberty of parents to direct the upbringing, education, and care of their children is a fundamental right."

Just as the Supreme Court sees the First Amendment as the source of our right to free speech, and they decide what speech is protected by that amendment and what speech is not, so it will see the PRA as the source of parental rights, and the judges will decide what rights parents have and what rights they do not have.

Do the words "upbringing" or "care" in Section 1 above include religious training, discipline, diet, medical treatment, and whether the child may wield a hoe in the family garden? What does it mean that these subjects are not listed? Does it mean that parents do not have rights regarding these issues? The Supreme Court will decide what it means.

> "Section 2: The parental right to direct education includes the right to choose public, private, religious, or home schools, and the right to make reasonable choices within public schools for one's child."

What is not included in the parental right to direct education? What is a "reasonable" choice? Who decides what is not included and what choices are "reasonable"? Federal judges decide.

> "Section 3: Neither the United States nor any State shall infringe these rights without demonstrating that its governmental interest as applied to the person is of the highest order and not otherwise served."

Whatever parental rights you think you have may be infringed upon by the federal government or the state governments if they have a good reason for it. Federal judges will decide whether the federal or state governments have a good reason to infringe upon your "parental rights".

> "Section 4: This article shall not be construed to apply to a parental action or decision that would end life."

Does this mean that parents retained the right to make these decisions? Or does it mean that the PRA does not protect that right, hence parents no longer have it?

What if federal courts construe this section to mean that parents will no longer be permitted to make decisions about terminating or continuing medical care for their ill, injured, or defective (Downs' syndrome, birth defects, etc.) children?

> "Section 5: No treaty may be adopted nor shall any source of international law be employed to supersede, modify, interpret, or apply to the rights guaranteed by this article."

No rights are guaranteed by the PRA. Not one parental right can be named that cannot be voided if the federal or state government shows federal judges that the government has an interest in voiding the right.

Furthermore, since the PRA makes federal control of children an enumerated power, it is the PRA itself which would give the U.S. Senate constitutional authority to ratify the U.N. Declaration on the Rights of the Child.

The Proposed 28th Amendment

The proposed 28th Amendment reads:

> "Congress shall make no law that applies to the citizens of the United States that does not apply equally to the Senators and/or Representatives; and, Congress shall make no law that applies to the Senators and/or Representatives that does not apply equally to the citizens of the United States."

Should we support this? How could any amendment make them obey the Constitution when they do not obey it now?

The proposed 28th Amendment would have the effect of creating a general legislative power in Congress. A general legislative power is the opposite of enumerated powers. With the general legislative power created by the proposed 28th Amendment, Congress could make any law on any subject as long as it applied to them as well as to us. They would no longer be constrained by the enumerated powers.

While some might think that the 28th Amendment will prevent Congress from exempting themselves, the actual result of such an amendment would destroy the concept of enumerated powers altogether.

Questions and Research Assignments

1. Paraphrase the following segment of James Madison's Federalist Paper No. 39:

> "If we try the Constitution by its last relation to the authority by which amendments are to be made, we find it neither wholly NATIONAL nor wholly FEDERAL. Were it wholly national, the supreme and ultimate authority would reside in the MAJORITY of the people of the Union; and this authority would be competent at all times, like that of a majority of every national society, to alter or abolish its established government. Were it wholly federal, on the other hand, the concurrence of each State in the Union would be essential to every alteration that would be binding on all. The mode provided by the plan of the convention is not founded on either of these principles. In requiring more than a majority, and principles. In requiring more than a majority, and particularly in computing the proportion by STATES, not by CITIZENS, it departs from the NATIONAL and advances towards the FEDERAL character; in rendering the concurrence of less than the whole number of States sufficient, it loses again the FEDERAL and partakes of the NATIONAL character.
>
> The proposed Constitution, therefore, is, in strictness, neither a national nor a federal Constitution, but a composition of both. In its foundation it is federal, not national; in the sources from which the ordinary powers of the government are drawn, it is partly federal and partly national; in the operation of these powers, it is national, not federal; in the extent of them, again, it is federal, not national; and, finally, in the authoritative mode of introducing amendments, it is neither wholly federal nor wholly national."

2. Paraphrase the following segment of Federalist Paper No. 62:

"The qualifications proposed for senators, as distinguished from those of representatives, consist in a more advanced age and a longer period of citizenship. A senator must be thirty years of age at least; as a representative must be twenty-five. And the former must have been a citizen nine years; as seven years are required for the latter. The propriety of these distinctions is explained by the nature of the senatorial trust, which, requiring greater extent of information and stability of character, requires at the same time that the senator should have reached a period of life most likely to supply these advantages; and which, participating immediately in transactions with foreign nations, ought to be exercised by none who are not thoroughly weaned from the prepossessions and habits incident to foreign birth and education. The term of nine years appears to be a prudent mediocrity between a total exclusion of adopted citizens, whose merits and talents may claim a share in the public confidence, and an indiscriminate and hasty admission of them, which might create a channel for foreign influence on the national councils. II. It is equally unnecessary to dilate on the appointment of senators by the State legislatures. Among the various modes which might have been devised for constituting this branch of the government, that which has been proposed by the convention is probably the most congenial with the public opinion. It is recommended by the double advantage of favoring a select appointment, and of giving to the State governments such an agency in the formation of the federal government as must secure the authority of the former, and may form a convenient link between the two systems."

3. Show why the below amendment should not be introduced and ratified.

"All Executive Branch regulations exceeding an economic burden of $100 million, as determined jointly by the Government Accountability Office and the Congressional Budget Office, shall be submitted to a permanent Joint Committee of Congress, hereafter the Congressional Delegation Oversight Committee, for review and approval prior to their implementation."

4. List the arguments against using a convention of the states to amend the Constitution even though permitted by Article V of the Constitution.

5. Why is a balanced budget amendment unnecessary? List the reasons why it would be a bad amendment to make to the Constitution.

6. What undesirable results would come about if the Electoral College was eliminated and the president chosen by popular vote?

REFERENCES

A. The Declaration of Independence.

B. The Constitution of the United States, including the amendments.

C. The Virginia and Kentucky Resolutions.

D. The Alien and Sedition Acts.

E. George Washington's Presidential Cabinet.

F. John Cornyn's Balance Budget Amendment.

G. Glossary.

H. Acknowlegements.

A. The Declaration of Independence

Transcript of Declaration of Independence (1776)

IN CONGRESS, July 4, 1776.

The unanimous Declaration of the thirteen united States of America,

WHEN in the Course of human Events, it becomes necessary for one People to dissolve the Political Bands which have connected them with another, and to assume among the Powers of the Earth, the separate and equal Station to which the Laws of Nature and of Nature's God entitle them, a decent Respect to the Opinions of Mankind requires that they should declare the causes which impel them to the Separation.

WE hold these Truths to be self-evident, that all Men are created equal, that they are endowed by their Creator with certain unalienable Rights, that among these are Life, Liberty, and the Pursuit of Happiness— That to secure these Rights, Governments are instituted among Men, deriving their just Powers from the Consent of the Governed, that whenever any form of Government becomes destructive of these Ends, it is the Right of the People to alter or to abolish it, and to institute new Government, laying its Foundation on such Principles, and organizing its Powers in such form, as to them shall seem most likely to effect their Safety and Happiness. Prudence, indeed, will dictate that Governments long established should not be changed for light and transient Causes; and accordingly all Experience hath shewn, that Mankind are more disposed to suffer, while Evils are sufferable, than to right themselves by abolishing the forms to which they are accustomed. But when a long Train of Abuses and Usurpations, pursuing invariably the same Object, evinces a Design to reduce them under absolute Despotism, it is their Right, it is their Duty, to throw off such Government, and to provide new Guards for their future Security. Such has been the patient Sufferance of these Colonies; and such is now the Necessity which constrains them to alter their former Systems of Government. The

History of the present King of Great Britain is a History of repeated Injuries and Usurpations, all having in direct Object the Establishment of an absolute Tyranny over these States. To prove this, let Facts be submitted to a candid World.

He has refused his Assent to Laws, the most wholesome and necessary for the public Good.

He has forbidden his Governors to pass Laws of immediate and pressing Importance, unless suspended in their Operation till his Assent should be obtained; and when so suspended, he has utterly neglected to attend to them.

He has refused to pass other Laws for the Accommodation of large Districts of People, unless those People would relinquish the Right of Representation in the Legislature, a Right inestimable to them, and formidable to Tyrants only.

He has called together Legislative Bodies at Places unusual, uncomfortable, and distant from the Depository of their public Records, for the sole Purpose of fatiguing them into Compliance with his Measures.

He has dissolved Representative Houses repeatedly, for opposing with manly Firmness his Invasions on the Rights of the People.

He has refused for a long Time, after such Dissolutions, to cause others to be elected; whereby the Legislative Powers, incapable of Annihilation, have returned to the People at large for their exercise; the State remaining in the mean time exposed to all the Dangers of Invasion from without, and Convulsions within.

He has endeavoured to prevent the Population of these States; for that Purpose obstructing the Laws for Naturalization of foreigners; refusing to pass others to encourage their Migrations hither, and raising the Conditions of new Appropriations of Lands.

He has obstructed the Administration of Justice, by refusing his assent to Laws for establishing Judiciary Powers.

He has made Judges dependent on his Will alone, for the Tenure of their Offices, and the Amount and Payment of their Salaries.

He has erected a Multitude of new Offices, and sent hither Swarms of Officers to harrass our People, and eat out their Substance.

He has kept among us, in Times of Peace, Standing Armies, without the consent of our Legislatures.

He has affected to render the Military independent of and superior to the Civil Power.

He has combined with others to subject us to a Jurisdiction foreign to our Constitution, and unacknowledged by our Laws; giving his Assent to their Acts of pretended Legislation:

For quartering large Bodies of Armed Troops among us:

For protecting them, by a mock Trial, from Punishment for any Murders which they should commit on the Inhabitants of these States:

For cutting off our Trade with all Parts of the World:

For imposing Taxes on us without our Consent:

For depriving us, in many Cases, of the Benefits of Trial by Jury:

For transporting us beyond Seas to be tried for pretended Offences:

For abolishing the free System of English Laws in a neighbouring Province, establishing therein an arbitrary Government and enlarging its Boundaries, so as to render it at once an Example and fit Instrument for introducing the same absolute Rule into these Colonies:

For taking away our Charters, abolishing our most valuable Laws, and altering fundamentally the forms of our Governments:

For suspending our own Legislatures, and declaring themselves invested with Power to legislate for us in all Cases whatsoever.

He has abdicated Government here, by declaring us out of his Protection and waging War against us.

He has plundered our Seas, ravaged our Coasts, burnt our Towns, and destroyed the Lives of our People.

He is, at this Time, transporting large Armies of foreign Mercenaries to compleat the Works of Death, Desolation, and Tyranny already begun with circumstances of Cruelty and Perfidy, scarcely paralleled in the most barbarous Ages, and totally unworthy of the Head of a civilized Nation.

He has constrained our fellow Citizens taken Captive on the high Seas to bear Arms against their Country, to become the Executioners of their friends and Brethren, or to fall themselves by their Hands.

He has excited domestic Insurrections amongst us, and has endeavoured to bring on the Inhabitants of our Frontiers, the merciless Indian Savages, whose known Rule of Warfare, is an undistinguished Destruction, of all Ages, Sexes and Conditions.

In every stage of these Oppressions we have Petitioned for Redress in the most humble Terms: Our repeated Petitions have been answered only by repeated Injury. A Prince, whose Character is thus marked by every act which may define a Tyrant, is unfit to be the Ruler of a free People.

Nor have we been wanting in Attentions to our British Brethren. We have warned them from Time to Time of Attempts by their Legislature to extend an unwarrantable jurisdiction over us. We have reminded them of the Circumstances of our Emigration and Settlement here. We have appealed to their native justice and Magnanimity, and we have conjured them by the Ties of our common Kindred to disavow these Usurpations, which, would inevitably interrupt our Connections and Correspondence. They too have been deaf to the Voice of Justice and of Consanguinity. We must, therefore, acquiesce in the Necessity, which denounces our Separation, and hold them, as we hold the rest of Mankind, Enemies in War, in Peace, Friends.

We, therefore, the Representatives of the UNITED STATES OF AMERICA, in General Congress, Assembled, appealing to the Supreme Judge of the World for the Rectitude of our Intentions, do, in the Name, and by Authority of the good People of these Colonies, solemnly Publish and Declare, That these United Colonies are, and of Right ought to be, FREE AND INDEPENDENT STATES, that they are absolved from all Allegiance to the British Crown, and that all political Connection between them and the State of Great Britain, is and ought to be totally dissolved; and that as FREE AND INDEPENDENT STATES, they have full Power to levy War, conclude Peace, contract Alliances, establish Commerce, and to do all other Acts and Things which INDEPENDENT STATES may of right do. And for the support of this Declaration, with a firm Reliance on the Protection of divine Providence, we mutually pledge to each other our Lives, our fortunes, and our sacred Honor.

B. The Constitution of the United States, including Amendments

Preamble

We the People of the United States, in Order to form a more perfect Union, establish Justice, insure domestic Tranquility, provide for the common defence, promote the general Welfare, and secure the Blessings of Liberty to ourselves and our Posterity, do ordain and establish this Constitution for the United States of America.

Article I

Section 1. All legislative Powers herein granted shall be vested in a Congress of the United States, which shall consist of a Senate and House of Representatives.

Section 2. The House of Representatives shall be composed of Members chosen every second Year by the People of the several States, and the Electors in each State shall have the Qualifications requisite for Electors of the most numerous Branch of the State Legislature.

No Person shall be a Representative who shall not have attained to the Age of twenty five Years, and been seven Years a Citizen of the United States, and who shall not, when elected, be an Inhabitant of that State in which he shall be chosen.

[Representatives and direct Taxes shall be apportioned among the several States which may be included within this Union, according to their respective Numbers, which shall be determined by adding to the whole Number of free Persons, including those bound to Service for a Term of Years, and excluding Indians not taxed, three fifths of all other Persons.]*[3]

---

[3]   Changed by section 2 of the Fourteenth Amendment

The actual Enumeration shall be made within three Years after the first Meeting of the Congress of the United States, and within every subsequent Term of ten Years, in such Manner as they shall by Law direct. The Number of Representatives shall not exceed one for every thirty Thousand, but each State shall have at Least one Representative; and until such enumeration shall be made, the State of New Hampshire shall be entitled to chuse three, Massachusetts eight, Rhode Island and Providence Plantations one, Connecticut five, New York six, New Jersey four, Pennsylvania eight, Delaware one, Maryland six, Virginia ten, North Carolina five, South Carolina five and Georgia three.

When vacancies happen in the Representation from any State, the Executive Authority thereof shall issue Writs of Election to fill such Vacancies.

The House of Representatives shall chuse their Speaker and other Officers; and shall have the sole Power of Impeachment.

Section 3. The Senate of the United States shall be composed of two Senator from each State, [chosen by the Legislature thereof,]*4 for six Years; and each Senator shall have one Vote.

Immediately after they shall be assembled in Consequence of the first Election, they shall be divided as equally as may be into three Classes. The Seats of the Senators of the first Class shall be vacated at the Expiration of the second Year, of the second Class at the Expiration of the fourth Year, and of the third Class at the Expiration of the sixth Year, so that one third may be chosen every second Year; [and if Vacancies happen by Resignation, or otherwise, during the Recess of the Legislature of any State, the Executive thereof may make temporary Appointments until the next Meeting of the Legislature, which shall then fill such Vacancies.]*5

No person shall be a Senator who shall not have attained to the Age of thirty Years, and been nine Years a Citizen of the United States, and

---

1   Changed by the Seventeenth Amendment
5   Changed by the Seventeenth Amendment

who shall not, when elected, be an Inhabitant of that State for which he shall be chosen.

The Vice President of the United States shall be President of the Senate, but shall have no Vote, unless they be equally divided.

The Senate shall chuse their other Officers, and also a President pro tempore, in the absence of the Vice President, or when he shall exercise the Office of President of the United States.

The Senate shall have the sole Power to try all Impeachments. When sitting for that Purpose, they shall be on Oath or Affirmation. When the President of the United States is tried, the Chief Justice shall preside: And no Person shall be convicted without the Concurrence of two thirds of the Members present.

Judgment in Cases of Impeachment shall not extend further than to removal from Office, and disqualification to hold and enjoy any Office of honor, Trust or Profit under the United States: but the Party convicted shall nevertheless be liable and subject to Indictment, Trial, Judgment and Punishment, according to Law.

Section 4. The Times, Places and Manner of holding Elections for Senators and Representatives, shall be prescribed in each State by the Legislature thereof; but the Congress may at any time by Law make or alter such Regulations, except as to the Place of Chusing Senators.

The Congress shall assemble at least once in every Year, and such Meeting shall [be on the first Monday in December,]*[6] unless they shall by Law appoint a different Day.

Section 5. Each House shall be the Judge of the Elections, Returns and Qualifications of its own Members, and a Majority of each shall constitute a Quorum to do Business; but a smaller number may adjourn from day to day, and may be authorized to compel the Attendance of

---

[6]   Changed by section 2 of the Twentieth Amendment

absent Members, in such Manner, and under such Penalties as each House may provide.

Each House may determine the Rules of its Proceedings, punish its Members for disorderly Behavior, and, with the Concurrence of two-thirds, expel a Member.

Each House shall keep a Journal of its Proceedings, and from time to time publish the same, excepting such Parts as may in their Judgment require Secrecy; and the Yeas and Nays of the Members of either House on any question shall, at the Desire of one fifth of those Present, be entered on the Journal.

Neither House, during the Session of Congress, shall, without the Consent of the other, adjourn for more than three days, nor to any other Place than that in which the two Houses shall be sitting.

Section 6. The Senators and Representatives shall receive a Compensation for their Services, to be ascertained by Law, and paid out of the Treasury of the United States. They shall in all Cases, except Treason, Felony and Breach of the Peace, be privileged from Arrest during their Attendance at the Session of their respective Houses, and in going to and returning from the same; and for any Speech or Debate in either House, they shall not be questioned in any other Place.

No Senator or Representative shall, during the Time for which he was elected, be appointed to any civil Office under the Authority of the United States which shall have been created, or the Emoluments whereof shall have been increased during such time; and no Person holding any Office under the United States, shall be a Member of either House during his Continuance in Office.

Section 7. All bills for raising Revenue shall originate in the House of Representatives; but the Senate may propose or concur with Amendments as on other Bills.

Every Bill which shall have passed the House of Representatives and the Senate, shall, before it become a Law, be presented to the President of the United States; If he approve he shall sign it, but if not he shall return it, with his Objections to that House in which it shall have originated, who shall enter the Objections at large on their Journal, and proceed to reconsider it. If after such Reconsideration two thirds of that House shall agree to pass the Bill, it shall be sent, together with the Objections, to the other House, by which it shall likewise be reconsidered, and if approved by two thirds of that House, it shall become a Law. But in all such Cases the Votes of both Houses shall be determined by Yeas and Nays, and the Names of the Persons voting for and against the Bill shall be entered on the Journal of each House respectively. If any Bill shall not be returned by the President within ten Days (Sundays excepted) after it shall have been presented to him, the Same shall be a Law, in like Manner as if he had signed it, unless the Congress by their Adjournment prevent its Return, in which Case it shall not be a Law.

Every Order, Resolution, or Vote to which the Concurrence of the Senate and House of Representatives may be necessary (except on a question of Adjournment) shall be presented to the President of the United States; and before the Same shall take Effect, shall be approved by him, or being disapproved by him, shall be repassed by two thirds of the Senate and House of Representatives, according to the Rules and Limitations prescribed in the Case of a Bill.

Section 8. The Congress shall have Power To lay and collect Taxes, Duties, Imposts and Excises, to pay the Debts and provide for the common Defence and general Welfare of the United States; but all Duties, Imposts and Excises shall be uniform throughout the United States;

To borrow money on the credit of the United States;

To regulate Commerce with foreign Nations, and among the several States, and with the Indian Tribes;

To establish an uniform Rule of Naturalization, and uniform Laws on the subject of Bankruptcies throughout the United States;

To coin Money, regulate the Value thereof, and of foreign Coin, and fix the Standard of Weights and Measures;

To provide for the Punishment of counterfeiting the Securities and current Coin of the United States;

To establish Post Offices and Post Roads;

To promote the Progress of Science and useful Arts, by securing for limited Times to Authors and Inventors the exclusive Right to their respective Writings and Discoveries;

To constitute Tribunals inferior to the supreme Court;

To define and punish Piracies and Felonies committed on the high Seas, and Offenses against the Law of Nations;

To declare War, grant Letters of Marque and Reprisal, and make Rules concerning Captures on Land and Water;

To raise and support Armies, but no Appropriation of Money to that Use shall be for a longer Term than two Years;

To provide and maintain a Navy;

To make Rules for the Government and Regulation of the land and naval Forces;

To provide for calling forth the Militia to execute the Laws of the Union, suppress Insurrections and repel Invasions; To provide for organizing, arming, and disciplining the Militia, and for governing such Part of them as may be employed in the Service of the United States, reserving to the States respectively, the Appointment of the Officers, and the Authority of training the Militia according to the discipline prescribed by Congress;

To exercise exclusive Legislation in all Cases whatsoever, over such District (not exceeding ten Miles square) as may, by Cession of particular States, and the acceptance of Congress, become the Seat of the Government of the United States, and to exercise like Authority over all Places purchased by the Consent of the Legislature of the State in which the Same shall be, for the Erection of Forts, Magazines, Arsenals, dock-Yards, and other needful Buildings; And

To make all Laws which shall be necessary and proper for carrying into Execution the foregoing Powers, and all other Powers vested by this Constitution in the Government of the United States, or in any Department or Officer thereof.

Section 9. The Migration or Importation of such Persons as any of the States now existing shall think proper to admit, shall not be prohibited by the Congress prior to the Year one thousand eight hundred and eight, but a tax or duty may be imposed on such Importation, not exceeding ten dollars for each Person.

The privilege of the Writ of Habeas Corpus shall not be suspended, unless when in Cases of Rebellion or Invasion the public Safety may require it.

No Bill of Attainder or ex post facto Law shall be passed.

[No capitation, or other direct, Tax shall be laid, unless in Proportion to the Census or Enumeration herein before directed to be taken.]*[7]

No Tax or Duty shall be laid on Articles exported from any State.

No Preference shall be given by any Regulation of Commerce or Revenue to the Ports of one State over those of another: nor shall Vessels bound to, or from, one State, be obliged to enter, clear, or pay Duties in another.

No Money shall be drawn from the Treasury, but in Consequence of Appropriations made by Law; and a regular Statement and Account of

---

[7]   See Sixteenth Amendment

the Receipts and Expenditures of all public Money shall be published from time to time.

No Title of Nobility shall be granted by the United States: And no Person holding any Office of Profit or Trust under them, shall, without the Consent of the Congress, accept of any present, Emolument, Office, or Title, of any kind whatever, from any King, Prince or foreign State.

Section 10. No State shall enter into any Treaty, Alliance, or Confederation; grant Letters of Marque and Reprisal; coin Money; emit Bills of Credit; make any Thing but gold and silver Coin a Tender in Payment of Debts; pass any Bill of Attainder, ex post facto Law, or Law impairing the Obligation of Contracts, or grant any Title of Nobility.

No State shall, without the Consent of the Congress, lay any Imposts or Duties on Imports or Exports, except what may be absolutely necessary for executing it's inspection Laws: and the net Produce of all Duties and Imposts, laid by any State on Imports or Exports, shall be for the Use of the Treasury of the United States; and all such Laws shall be subject to the Revision and Controul of the Congress.

No State shall, without the Consent of Congress, lay any duty of Tonnage, keep Troops, or Ships of War in time of Peace, enter into any Agreement or Compact with another State, or with a foreign Power, or engage in War, unless actually invaded, or in such imminent Danger as will not admit of delay.

Article II

Section 1. The executive Power shall be vested in a President of the United States of America. He shall hold his Office during the Term of four Years, and, together with the Vice-President chosen for the same Term, be elected, as follows:

Each State shall appoint, in such Manner as the Legislature thereof may direct, a Number of Electors, equal to the whole Number of Senators and Representatives to which the State may be entitled in the Congress:

but no Senator or Representative, or Person holding an Office of Trust or Profit under the United States, shall be appointed an Elector.

[The Electors shall meet in their respective States, and vote by Ballot for two persons, of whom one at least shall not lie an Inhabitant of the same State with themselves. And they shall make a List of all the Persons voted for, and of the Number of Votes for each; which List they shall sign and certify, and transmit sealed to the Seat of the Government of the United States, directed to the President of the Senate. The President of the Senate shall, in the Presence of the Senate and House of Representatives, open all the Certificates, and the Votes shall then be counted. The Person having the greatest Number of Votes shall be the President, if such Number be a Majority of the whole Number of Electors appointed; and if there be more than one who have such Majority, and have an equal Number of Votes, then the House of Representatives shall immediately chuse by Ballot one of them for President; and if no Person have a Majority, then from the five highest on the List the said House shall in like Manner chuse the President. But in chusing the President, the Votes shall be taken by States, the representation from each State having one Vote; a quorum for this Purpose shall consist of a Member or Members from two-thirds of the States, and a Majority of all the States shall be necessary to a Choice. In every Case, after the Choice of the President, the Person having the greatest Number of Votes of the Electors shall be the Vice President. But if there should remain two or more who have equal Votes, the Senate shall chuse from them by Ballot the Vice-President.]*[8]

The Congress may determine the Time of chusing the Electors, and the Day on which they shall give their Votes; which Day shall be the same throughout the United States.

No person except a natural born Citizen, or a Citizen of the United States, at the time of the Adoption of this Constitution, shall be eligible to the Office of President; neither shall any Person be eligible to that Office who shall not have attained to the Age of thirty-five Years, and been fourteen Years a Resident within the United States.

---

[8]   Changed by the Twelfth Amendment

[In Case of the Removal of the President from Office, or of his Death, Resignation, or Inability to discharge the Powers and Duties of the said Office, the same shall devolve on the Vice President, and the Congress may by Law provide for the Case of Removal, Death, Resignation or Inability, both of the President and Vice President, declaring what Officer shall then act as President, and such Officer shall act accordingly, until the Disability be removed, or a President shall be elected.]*[9]

The President shall, at Stated Times, receive for his Services, a Compensation, which shall neither be increased nor diminished during the Period for which he shall have been elected, and he shall not receive within that Period any other Emolument from the United States, or any of them.

Before he enter on the Execution of his Office, he shall take the following Oath or Affirmation: "I do solemnly swear (or affirm) that I will faithfully execute the Office of President of the United States, and will to the best of my Ability, preserve, protect and defend the Constitution of the United States."

Section 2. The President shall be Commander in Chief of the Army and Navy of the United States, and of the Militia of the several States, when called into the actual Service of the United States; he may require the Opinion, in writing, of the principal Officer in each of the executive Departments, upon any subject relating to the Duties of their respective Offices, and he shall have Power to Grant Reprieves and Pardons for Offenses against the United States, except in Cases of Impeachment.

He shall have Power, by and with the Advice and Consent of the Senate, to make Treaties, provided two thirds of the Senators present concur; and he shall nominate, and by and with the Advice and Consent of the Senate, shall appoint Ambassadors, other public Ministers and Consuls, Judges of the supreme Court, and all other Officers of the United States, whose Appointments are not herein otherwise provided for, and which shall be established by Law: but the Congress may

---

[9]   Changed by the Twenty-fifth Amendment

by Law vest the Appointment of such inferior Officers, as they think proper, in the President alone, in the Courts of Law, or in the Heads of Departments.

The President shall have Power to fill up all Vacancies that may happen during the Recess of the Senate, by granting Commissions which shall expire at the End of their next Session.

Section 3. He shall from time to time give to the Congress Information of the State of the Union, and recommend to their Consideration such Measures as he shall judge necessary and

expedient; he may, on extraordinary Occasions, convene both Houses, or either of them, and in Case of Disagreement between them, with Respect to the Time of Adjournment, he may adjourn them to such Time as he shall think proper; he shall receive Ambassadors and other public Ministers; he shall take Care that the Laws be faithfully executed, and shall Commission all the Officers of the United States.

Section 4. The President, Vice President and all civil Officers of the United States, shall be removed from Office on Impeachment for, and Conviction of, Treason, Bribery, or other high Crimes and Misdemeanors.

Article III

Section 1. The judicial Power of the United States, shall be vested in one supreme Court, and in such inferior Courts as the Congress may from time to time ordain and establish. The Judges, both of the supreme and inferior Courts, shall hold their Offices during good Behavior, and shall, at Stated Times, receive for their Services a Compensation which shall not be diminished during their Continuance in Office.

Section 2. [The judicial Power shall extend to all Cases, in Law and Equity, arising under this Constitution, the Laws of the United States, and Treaties made, or which shall be made, under their Authority; to all Cases affecting Ambassadors, other public Ministers and Consuls; to all Cases of admiralty and maritime Jurisdiction; to Controversies to which

THE HANDBOOK FOR WE THE PEOPLE

the United States shall be a Party; to Controversies between two or more States; between a State and Citizens of another State; between Citizens of different States; between Citizens of the same State claiming Lands under Grants of different States, and between a State, or the Citizens thereof, and foreign States, Citizens or Subjects.]*[10]

In all Cases affecting Ambassadors, other public Ministers and Consuls, and those in which a State shall be Party, the supreme Court shall have original Jurisdiction. In all the other Cases before mentioned, the supreme Court shall have appellate Jurisdiction, both as to Law and Fact, with such Exceptions, and under such Regulations as the Congress shall make.

The Trial of all Crimes, except in Cases of Impeachment, shall be by Jury; and such Trial shall be held in the State where the said Crimes shall have been committed; but when not committed within any State, the Trial shall be at such Place or Places as the Congress may by Law have directed.

Section 3. Treason against the United States, shall consist only in levying War against them, or in adhering to their Enemies, giving them Aid and Comfort. No Person shall be convicted of Treason unless on the Testimony of two Witnesses to the same overt Act, or on Confession in open Court.

The Congress shall have power to declare the Punishment of Treason, but no Attainder of Treason shall work Corruption of Blood, or Forfeiture except during the Life of the Person attainted.

Article IV

Section 1. Full Faith and Credit shall be given in each State to the public Acts, Records, and judicial Proceedings of every other State. And the Congress may by general Laws prescribe the Manner in which such Acts, Records and Proceedings shall be proved, and the Effect thereof.

---

[10]   Changed by the Eleventh Amendment

Section 2. The Citizens of each State shall be entitled to all Privileges and Immunities of Citizens in the several States.

A Person charged in any State with Treason, Felony, or other Crime, who shall flee from Justice, and be found in another State, shall on demand of the executive Authority of the State from which he fled, be delivered up, to be removed to the State having Jurisdiction of the Crime.

[No Person held to Service or Labour in one State, under the Laws thereof, escaping into another, shall, in Consequence of any Law or Regulation therein, be discharged from such Service or Labour, But shall be delivered up on Claim of the Party to whom such Service or Labour may be due.]*[11]

Section 3. New States may be admitted by the Congress into this Union; but no new States shall be formed or erected within the Jurisdiction of any other State; nor any State be formed by the Junction of two or more States, or parts of States, without the consent of the Legislatures of the States concerned as well as of the Congress.

The Congress shall have Power to dispose of and make all needful Rules and Regulations respecting the Territory or other Property belonging to the United States; and nothing in this Constitution shall be so construed as to Prejudice any Claims of the United States, or of any particular State.

Section 4. The United States shall guarantee to every State in this Union a Republican Form of Government, and shall protect each of them against Invasion; and on Application of the Legislature, or of the Executive (when the Legislature cannot be convened) against domestic Violence.

Article V

The Congress, whenever two thirds of both Houses shall deem it necessary, shall propose Amendments to this Constitution, or, on the

---

[11]   Changed by the Thirteenth Amendment

Application of the Legislatures of two thirds of the several States, shall call a Convention for proposing Amendments, which, in either Case, shall be valid to all Intents and Purposes, as part of this Constitution, when ratified by the Legislatures of three fourths of the several States, or by Conventions in three fourths thereof, as the one or the other Mode of Ratification may be proposed by the Congress; Provided that no Amendment which may be made prior to the Year One thousand eight hundred and eight shall in any Manner affect the first and fourth Clauses in the Ninth Section of the first Article; and that no State, without its Consent, shall be deprived of its equal Suffrage in the Senate.

Article VI

All Debts contracted and Engagements entered into, before the Adoption of this Constitution, shall be as valid against the United States under this Constitution, as under the Confederation.

This Constitution, and the Laws of the United States which shall be made in Pursuance thereof; and all Treaties made, or which shall be made, under the Authority of the United States, shall be the supreme Law of the Land; and the Judges in every State shall be bound thereby, any Thing in the Constitution or Laws of any State to the Contrary notwithstanding.

The Senators and Representatives before mentioned, and the Members of the several State Legislatures, and all executive and judicial Officers, both of the United States and of the several States, shall be bound by Oath or Affirmation, to support this Constitution; but no religious Test shall ever be required as a Qualification to any Office or public Trust under the United States.

Article VII

The Ratification of the Conventions of nine States, shall be sufficient for the Establishment of this Constitution between the States so ratifying the Same.

Done in Convention by the Unanimous Consent of the States present the Seventeenth Day of September in the Year of our Lord one thousand seven hundred and Eighty seven and of the Independence of the United States of America the Twelfth. In Witness whereof We have hereunto subscribed our Names.

George Washington - President and deputy from Virginia
New Hampshire - John Langdon, Nicholas Gilman
Massachusetts - Nathaniel Gorham, Rufus King
Connecticut - Wm. Saml. Johnson, Roger Sherman
New York - Alexander Hamilton
New Jersey - Wil Livingston, David Brearley, Wm Paterson, Jona. Dayton
Pennsylvania - B Franklin, Thomas Mifflin, Robt Morris, Geo. Clymer, Thos FitzSimons,
Jared Ingersoll, James Wilson, Gouv Morris
Delaware - Geo. Read, Gunning Bedford jun, John Dickinson, Richard Bassett, Jaco. Broom
Maryland - James McHenry, Dan of St Tho Jenifer, Danl Carroll
Virginia - John Blair, James Madison Jr.
North Carolina - Wm Blount, Richd Dobbs Spaight, Hu Williamson
South Carolina - J. Rutledge, Charles Cotesworth Pinckney, Charles Pinckney, Pierce Butler
Georgia - William Few, Abr Baldwin
Attest: William Jackson, Secretary

The Amendments

On September 25, 1789, Congress transmitted to the state legislatures twelve proposed amendments, two of which had to do with Congressional representation and Congressional pay, were not adopted. The remaining ten amendments became known as the Bill of Rights and were ratified Dec. 15, 1791.

Lesser known is the below *Preamble*. The importance in this is when told, for example, that the second amendment prevents the states from passing laws regulating guns, rifles, ammunition, this Preamble makes it clear the founders intended these first ten amendments to apply *only* to the newly-formed central government; not the states. The states are free to pass legislation that would restrict arms. A good example is states may pass legislation restricting arms to citizens who have a mental history, or they may pass legislation against free speech such prohibiting the shouting of "fire!" in a crowded theater. The founders expected by putting these decisions in the hands of the states rather than the central government, laws made on these subjects were much closer to the voters.

Preamble

Congress OF THE United States begun and held at the City of New York, on Wednesday the Fourth of March, one thousand seven hundred and eighty nine.

THE Conventions of a number of the States having at the time of their adopting the Constitution, expressed a desire, in order to prevent misconstruction or abuse of its powers, that further declaratory and restrictive clauses should be added: And as extending the ground of public confidence in the Government, will best insure the beneficent ends of its institution

RESOLVED by the Senate and House of Representatives of the United States of America, in Congress assembled, two thirds of both Houses concurring, that the following Articles be proposed to the Legislatures of the several States, as Amendments to the Constitution of the United States, all or any of which Articles, when ratified by three fourths of the said Legislatures, to be valid to all intents and purposes, as part of the said Constitution; viz.

ARTICLES in addition to, and Amendment of the Constitution of the United States of America, proposed by Congress, and ratified by the Legislatures of the several States, pursuant to the fifth Article of the original Constitution.

Amendment I

Congress shall make no law respecting an establishment of religion, or prohibiting the free exercise thereof; or abridging the freedom of speech, or of the press; or the right of the people peaceably to assemble, and to petition the Government for a redress of grievances.

Amendment II

A well regulated Militia, being necessary to the security of a free State, the right of the people to keep and bear Arms, shall not be infringed.

Amendment III

No Soldier shall, in time of peace be quartered in any house, without the consent of the Owner, nor in time of war, but in a manner to be prescribed by law.

Amendment IV

The right of the people to be secure in their persons, houses, papers, and effects, against unreasonable searches and seizures, shall not be violated, and no Warrants shall issue, but upon probable cause, supported by Oath or affirmation, and particularly describing the place to be searched, and the persons or things to be seized.

Amendment V

No person shall be held to answer for a capital, or otherwise infamous crime, unless on a presentment or indictment of a Grand Jury, except in cases arising in the land or naval forces, or in the Militia, when in actual service in time of War or public danger; nor shall any person be subject for the same offense to be twice put in jeopardy of life or limb; nor shall be compelled in any criminal case to be a witness against himself, nor be deprived of life, liberty, or property, without due process of law; nor shall private property be taken for public use, without just compensation.

Amendment VI

In all criminal prosecutions, the accused shall enjoy the right to a speedy and public trial, by an impartial jury of the State and district wherein the crime shall have been committed, which district shall have been previously ascertained by law, and to be informed of the nature and cause of the accusation; to be confronted with the witnesses against him; to have compulsory process for obtaining witnesses in his favor, and to have the Assistance of Counsel for his defence.

Amendment VII

In Suits at common law, where the value in controversy shall exceed twenty dollars, the right of trial by jury shall be preserved, and no fact tried by a jury, shall be otherwise re-examined in any Court of the United States, than according to the rules of the common law.

Amendment VIII

Excessive bail shall not be required, nor excessive fines imposed, nor cruel and unusual punishments inflicted.

Amendment IX

The enumeration in the Constitution, of certain rights, shall not be construed to deny or disparage others retained by the people.

Amendment X

The powers not delegated to the United States by the Constitution, nor prohibited by it to the States, are reserved to the States respectively, or to the people.

Amendment XI

The Judicial power of the United States shall not be construed to extend to any suit in law or equity, commenced or prosecuted against one of the United States by Citizens of another State, or by Citizens or Subjects of any Foreign State.

Amendment XII

The Electors shall meet in their respective States, and vote by ballot for President and Vice-President, one of whom, at least, shall not be an inhabitant of the same State with themselves; they shall name in their ballots the person voted for as President, and in distinct ballots the person voted for as Vice-President, and they shall make distinct lists of all persons voted for as President, and of all persons voted for as Vice-President and of the number of votes for each, which lists they shall sign and certify, and transmit sealed to the seat of the government of the United States, directed to the President of the Senate;–The President of the Senate shall, in the presence of the Senate and House of Representatives, open all the certificates and the votes shall then be counted; –The person having the greatest Number of votes for President, shall be the President, if such number be a majority of the whole number of Electors appointed; and if no person have such majority, then from the persons having the highest numbers not exceeding three on the list of those voted for as President, the House of Representatives shall choose immediately, by ballot, the President. But in choosing the President, the votes shall be taken by States, the representation from each State having one vote; a quorum for this purpose shall consist of a member or members from two-thirds of the States, and a majority of all the States shall be necessary to a choice. [And if the House of Representatives shall not choose a President whenever the right of choice shall devolve upon them, before the fourth day of March next following, then the Vice-President shall act as President, as in the case of the death or other constitutional disability of the President.]*[12] The person having the greatest number of votes as Vice-President, shall be the Vice-President, if such number be a majority of the whole number of Electors appointed, and if no person have a majority, then from the two highest numbers on the list, the Senate shall choose the Vice-President; a quorum for the purpose shall consist of two-thirds of the whole number of Senators, and a majority of the whole number shall be necessary to a choice. But no person constitutionally ineligible to the office of President shall be eligible to that of Vice-President of the United States.

Amendment XIII

Section 1. Neither slavery nor involuntary servitude, except as a punishment for crime whereof the party shall have been duly convicted,

---

[12]   Superseded by section 3 of the Twentieth Amendment

shall exist within the United States, or any place subject to their jurisdiction.

Section 2. Congress shall have power to enforce this article by appropriate legislation.

Amendment XIV

Section 1. All persons born or naturalized in the United States, and subject to the jurisdiction thereof, are citizens of the United States and of the State wherein they reside. No State shall make or enforce any law which shall abridge the privileges or immunities of citizens of the United States; nor shall any State deprive any person of life, liberty, or property, without due process of law; nor deny to any person within its jurisdiction the equal protection of the laws.

Section 2. Representatives shall be apportioned among the several States according to their respective numbers, counting the whole number of persons in each State, excluding Indians not taxed. But when the right to vote at any election for the choice of electors for President and Vice-President of the United States, Representatives in Congress, the Executive and Judicial officers of a State, or the members of the Legislature thereof, is denied to any of the male inhabitants of such State , being twenty-one years of age, and citizens of the United States, or in any way abridged, except for participation in rebellion, or other crime, the basis of representation therein shall be reduced in the proportion which the number of such male citizens shall bear to the whole number of male citizens twenty-one years of age in such State.

Section 3. No person shall be a Senator or Representative in Congress, or elector of President and Vice-President, or hold any office, civil or military, under the United States, or under any State, who, having previously taken an oath, as a member of Congress, or as an officer of the United States, or as a member of any State legislature, or as an executive or judicial officer of any State, to support the Constitution of the United States, shall have engaged in insurrection or rebellion against the same, or given aid or comfort to the enemies thereof. But Congress may by a vote of two-thirds of each House, remove such disability.

Section 4. The validity of the public debt of the United States, authorized by law, including debts incurred for payment of pensions and bounties for services in suppressing insurrection or rebellion, shall not be questioned. But neither the United States nor any State shall assume or pay any debt or obligation incurred in aid of insurrection or rebellion against the United States, or any claim for the loss or emancipation of any slave; but all such debts, obligations and claims shall be held illegal and void.

Section 5. The Congress shall have power to enforce, by appropriate legislation, the provisions of this article.

Amendment XV

Section 1. The right of citizens of the United States to vote shall not be denied or abridged by the United States or by any State on account of race, color, or previous condition of servitude.

Section 2. The Congress shall have power to enforce this article by appropriate legislation.

Amendment XVI

The Congress shall have power to lay and collect taxes on incomes, from whatever source derived, without apportionment among the several States, and without regard to any census or enumeration.

Amendment XVII

The Senate of the United States shall be composed of two Senators from each State, elected by the people thereof, for six years; and each Senator shall have one vote. The electors in each State shall have the qualifications requisite for electors of the most numerous branch of the State legislatures.

When vacancies happen in the representation of any State in the Senate, the executive authority of such State shall issue writs of election to fill such vacancies: Provided, That the legislature of any State may empower the executive thereof to make temporary appointments until the people fill the vacancies by election as the legislature may direct.

This amendment shall not be so construed as to affect the election or term of any Senator chosen before it becomes valid as part of the Constitution.

Amendment XVIII*[13]

Section 1. After one year from the ratification of this article the manufacture, sale, or transportation of intoxicating liquors within, the importation thereof into, or the exportation thereof from the United States and all territory subject to the jurisdiction thereof for beverage purposes is hereby prohibited.

Section 2. The Congress and the several States shall have concurrent power to enforce this article by appropriate legislation.

Section 3. This article shall be inoperative unless it shall have been ratified as an amendment to the Constitution by the legislatures of the several States, as provided in the Constitution, within seven years from the date of the submission hereof to the States by the Congress.

Amendment XIX

The right of citizens of the United States to vote shall not be denied or abridged by the United States or by any State on account of sex.

Congress shall have power to enforce this article by appropriate legislation.

Amendment XX

Section 1. The terms of the President and Vice President shall end at noon on the 20th day of January, and the terms of Senators and Representatives at noon on the 3d day of January, of the years in which such terms would have ended if this article had not been ratified; and the terms of their successors shall then begin.

---

[13]   Repealed by the Twenty-first Amendment

Section 2. The Congress shall assemble at least once in every year, and such meeting shall begin at noon on the 3d day of January, unless they shall by law appoint a different day.

Section 3. If, at the time fixed for the beginning of the term of the President, the President elect shall have died, the Vice President elect shall become President. If a President shall not have been chosen before the time fixed for the beginning of his term, or if the President elect shall have failed to qualify, then the Vice President elect shall act as President until a President shall have qualified; and the Congress may by law provide for the case wherein neither a President elect nor a Vice President elect shall have qualified, declaring who shall then act as President, or the manner in which one who is to act shall be selected, and such person shall act accordingly until a President or Vice President shall have qualified.

Section 4. The Congress may by law provide for the case of the death of any of the persons from whom the House of Representatives may choose a President whenever the right of choice shall have devolved upon them, and for the case of the death of any of the persons from whom the Senate may choose a Vice President whenever the right of choice shall have devolved upon them.

Section 5. Sections 1 and 2 shall take effect on the 15th day of October following the ratification of this article.

Section 6. This article shall be inoperative unless it shall have been ratified as an amendment to the Constitution by the legislatures of three-fourths of the several States within seven years from the date of its submission.

Amendment XXI

Section 1. The eighteenth article of amendment to the Constitution of the United States is hereby repealed.

Section 2. The transportation or importation into any State, Territory, or possession of the United States for delivery or use therein of intoxicating liquors, in violation of the laws thereof, is hereby prohibited.

Section 3. The article shall be inoperative unless it shall have been ratified as an amendment to the Constitution by conventions in the several States, as provided in the Constitution, within seven years from the date of the submission hereof to the States by the Congress.

Amendment XXII

Section 1. No person shall be elected to the office of the President more than twice, and no person who has held the office of President, or acted as President, for more than two years of a term to which some other person was elected President shall be elected to the office of the President more than once. But this Article shall not apply to any person holding the office of President, when this Article was proposed by the Congress, and shall not prevent any person who may be holding the office of President, or acting as President, during the term within which this Article becomes operative from holding the office of President or acting as President during the remainder of such term.

Section 2. This article shall be inoperative unless it shall have been ratified as an amendment to the Constitution by the legislatures of three-fourths of the several States within seven years from the date of its submission to the States by the Congress.

Amendment XXIII

Section 1. The District constituting the seat of Government of the United States shall appoint in such manner as the Congress may direct: A number of electors of President and Vice President equal to the whole number of Senators and Representatives in Congress to which the District would be entitled if it were a State, but in no event more than the least populous State; they shall be in addition to those appointed by the States, but they shall be considered, for the purposes of the election of President and Vice President, to be electors appointed by a State; and they shall meet in the District and perform such duties as provided by the twelfth article of amendment.

Section 2. The Congress shall have power to enforce this article by appropriate legislation.

Amendment XXIV

Section 1. The right of citizens of the United States to vote in any primary or other election for President or Vice President, for electors for President or Vice President, or for Senator or Representative in Congress, shall not be denied or abridged by the United States or any State by reason of failure to pay any poll tax or other tax.

Section 2. The Congress shall have power to enforce this article by appropriate legislation

Amendment XXV

Section 1. In case of the removal of the President from office or of his death or resignation, the Vice President shall become President.

Section 2. Whenever there is a vacancy in the office of the Vice President, the President shall nominate a Vice President who shall take office upon confirmation by a majority vote of both Houses of Congress.

Section 3. Whenever the President transmits to the President pro tempore of the Senate and the Speaker of the House of Representatives his written declaration that he is unable to discharge the powers and duties of his office, and until he transmits to them a written declaration to the contrary, such powers and duties shall be discharged by the Vice President as Acting President.

Section 4. Whenever the Vice President and a majority of either the principal officers of the executive departments or of such other body as Congress may by law provide, transmit to the President pro tempore of the Senate and the Speaker of the House of Representatives their written declaration that the President is unable to discharge the powers and duties of his office, the Vice President shall immediately assume the powers and duties of the office as Acting President.

Thereafter, when the President transmits to the President pro tempore of the Senate and the Speaker of the House of Representatives his written declaration that no inability exists, he shall resume the powers and duties of his office unless the Vice President and a majority of either the principal officers of the executive department or of such other body as Congress may by law provide, transmit within four days to the President pro tempore of the Senate and the Speaker of the House of Representatives their written declaration that the President is unable to discharge the powers and duties of his office. Thereupon Congress shall decide the issue, assembling within forty eight hours for that purpose if not in session. If the Congress, within twenty one days after receipt of the latter written declaration, or, if Congress is not in session, within twenty one days after Congress is required to assemble, determines by two thirds vote of both Houses that the President is unable to discharge the powers and duties of his office, the Vice President shall continue to discharge the same as Acting President; otherwise, the President shall resume the powers and duties of his office.

Amendment XXVI

Section 1. The right of citizens of the United States, who are eighteen years of age or older, to vote shall not be denied or abridged by the United States or by any State on account of age.

Section 2. The Congress shall have power to enforce this article by appropriate legislation.

Amendment XXVII

No law, varying the compensation for the services of the Senators and Representatives, shall take effect, until an election of Representatives shall have intervened.

C. The Virginia and Kentucky Resolutions

The following resolution was adopted by the Virginia Senate on December 24, 1798, as a protest against the Alien and Sedition Acts passed by Congress. It was authored by James Madison, in collaboration with Thomas Jefferson, who authored a set of resolutions for Kentucky.

Virginia Resolution of 1798

RESOLVED, That the General Assembly of Virginia, doth unequivocally express a firm resolution to maintain and defend the Constitution of the United States, and the Constitution of this State, against every aggression either foreign or domestic, and that they will support the government of the United States in all measures warranted by the former.

That this assembly most solemnly declares a warm attachment to the Union of the States, to maintain which it pledges all its powers; and that for this end, it is their duty to watch over and oppose every infraction of those principles which constitute the only basis of that Union, because a faithful observance of them, can alone secure its existence and the public happiness.

That this Assembly doth explicitly and peremptorily declare, that it views the powers of the federal government, as resulting from the compact, to which the States are parties; as limited by the plain sense and intention of the instrument constituting the compact; as no further valid that they are authorized by the grants enumerated in that compact; and that in case of a deliberate, palpable, and dangerous exercise of other powers, not granted by the said compact, the States who are parties thereto, have the right, and are in duty bound, to interpose for arresting the progress of the evil, and for maintaining within their respective limits, the authorities, rights and liberties appertaining to them.

That the General Assembly doth also express its deep regret, that a spirit has in sundry instances, been manifested by the federal government, to enlarge its powers by forced constructions of the constitutional charter which defines them; and that implications have appeared of a design to expound certain general phrases (which having been copied from the very limited grant of power, in the former articles of confederation were the less liable to be misconstrued) so as to destroy the meaning and effect, of the particular enumeration which necessarily explains and limits the general phrases; and so as to consolidate the States by degrees, into one sovereignty, the obvious tendency and inevitable consequence of which would be, to transform the present republican system of the United States, into an absolute, or at best a mixed monarchy.

That the General Assembly doth particularly protest against the palpable and alarming infractions of the Constitution, in the two late cases of the "Alien and Sedition Acts" passed at the last session of Congress; the first of which exercises a power nowhere delegated to the federal government, and which by uniting legislative and judicial powers to those of executive, subverts the general principles of free government; as well as the particular organization, and positive provisions of the federal constitution; and the other of which acts, exercises in like manner, a power not delegated by the constitution, but on the contrary, expressly and positively forbidden by one of the amendments thereto; a power, which more than any other, ought to produce universal alarm, because it is leveled against that right of freely examining public characters and measures, and of free communication among the people thereon, which has ever been justly deemed, the only effectual guardian of every other right.

That this State having by its Convention, which ratified the federal Constitution, expressly declared, that among other essential rights, "the Liberty of Conscience and of the Press cannot be cancelled, abridged, restrained, or modified by any authority of the United States," and from its extreme anxiety to guard these rights from every possible attack of sophistry or ambition, having with other States, recommended an amendment for that purpose, which amendment was, in due time, annexed to the Constitution; it would mark a reproachable inconsistency, and criminal degeneracy, if an indifference were now shown, to the most palpable violation of one of the Rights, thus declared and secured; and to the establishment of a precedent which may be fatal to the other.

That the good people of this commonwealth, having ever felt, and continuing to feel, the most sincere affection for their brethren of the other States; the truest anxiety for establishing and perpetuating the union of all; and the most scrupulous fidelity to that constitution, which is the pledge of mutual friendship, and the instrument of mutual happiness; the General Assembly doth solemnly appeal to the like dispositions of the other States, in confidence that they will concur with this commonwealth in declaring, as it does hereby declare, that the acts aforesaid, are unconstitutional; and that the necessary and proper measures will be taken by each, for co-operating with this State, in maintaining the Authorities, Rights, and Liberties, referred to the States respectively, or to the people.

That the Governor be desired, to transmit a copy of the foregoing Resolutions to the executive authority of each of the other States, with a request that the same may be communicated to the Legislature thereof; and that a copy be furnished to each of the Senators and Representatives representing this State in the Congress of the United States.

Agreed to by the Senate, December 24, 1798.

KENTUCKY RESOLUTIONS OF 1798 AND 1799

[THE ORIGINAL DRAFT PREPARED BY THOMAS JEFFERSON.]

[The following Resolutions passed the House of Representatives of Kentucky, Nov. 10, 1798. On the passage of the 1st Resolution, one dissentient; 2d, 3d, 4th, 5th, 6th, 7th, 8th, two dissentients; 9th, three dissentients.]

1. Resolved, That the several States composing the United States of America are not united on the principle of unlimited submission to their general government; but that, by compact, under the style and title of a Constitution for the United States, and of amendments thereto, they constituted a general government for special purposes, delegated to that government certain definite powers, reserving, each State to itself, the residuary mass of right to their own self-government; and that whensoever the general government assumes undelegated powers, its acts are unauthoritative, void, and of no force; that to this compact each State acceded as a State, and is an integral party; that this government, created by this compact, was not made the exclusive or final judge of the extent of the powers delegated to itself, since that would have made its discretion, and not the Constitution, the measure of its powers; but that, as in all other cases of compact among powers having no common judge, each party has an equal right to judge for itself, as well of infractions as of the mode and measure of redress.

2. Resolved, That the Constitution of the United States having delegated to Congress a power to punish treason, counterfeiting the securities and current coin of the United States, piracies and felonies committed on the high seas, and offences against the laws of nations, and no other crimes, whatsoever; and it being true, as a general principle, and one of the amendments to the Constitution having also declared, that "the powers not delegated to the United States by the Constitution, nor prohibited by it to the States, are reserved to the States respectively, or to the people,"—therefore, also, the same act of Congress, passed on the 14th day of July, 1798, and entitled "An Act in Addition to the Act entitled 'An Act for the Punishment of certain Crimes against the United States;'" as also the act passed by them

on the 27th day of June, 1798, entitled "An Act to punish Frauds committed on the Bank of the United States," (and all other their acts which assume to create, define, or punish crimes other than those so enumerated in the Constitution,) are altogether void, and of no force; and that the power to create, define, and punish, such other crimes is reserved, and of right appertains, solely and exclusively, to the respective States, each within its own territory.

3. Resolved, That it is true, as a general principle, and is also expressly declared by one of the amendments to the Constitution, that "the powers not delegated to the United States by the Constitution, nor prohibited by it to the States, are reserved to the States respectively, or to the people;" and that, no power over the freedom of religion, freedom of speech, or freedom of the press, being delegated to the United States by the Constitution, nor prohibited by it to the States, all lawful powers respecting the same did of right remain, and were reserved to the States, or the people; that thus was manifested their determination to retain to themselves the right of judging how far the licentiousness of speech, and of the press, may be abridged without lessening their useful freedom, and how far those abuses which cannot be separated from their use, should be tolerated rather than the use be destroyed; and thus also they guarded against all abridgment, by the United States, of the freedom of religious principles and exercises, and retained to themselves the right of protecting the same, as this, Stated by a law passed on the general demand of its citizens, had already protected them from all human restraint or interference; and that, in addition to this general principle and express declaration, another and more special provision has been made by one of the amendments to the Constitution, which expressly declares, that "Congress shall make no law respecting an establishment of religion, or prohibiting the free exercise thereof, or abridging the freedom of speech, or of the press," thereby guarding, in the same sentence, and under the same words, the freedom of religion, of speech, and of the press, insomuch that whatever violated either throws down the sanctuary which covers the others,— and that libels, falsehood, and defamation, equally with heresy and false religion, are withheld from the cognizance of federal tribunals. That therefore the act of Congress of the United States, passed on the 14th of July, 1798, entitled "An Act in Addition to the Act entitled

'An Act for the Punishment of certain Crimes against the United States,'" which does abridge the freedom of the press, is not law, but is altogether void, and of no force.

4. Resolved, That alien friends are under the jurisdiction and protection of the laws of the State wherein they are; that no power over them has been delegated to the United States, nor prohibited to the individual States, distinct from their power over citizens; and it being true, as a general principle, and one of the amendments to the Constitution having also declared, that "the powers not delegated to the United States by the Constitution, nor prohibited by it to the States, are reserved to the States, respectively, or to the people," the act of the Congress of the United States, passed on the 22d day of July, 1798, entitled "An Act concerning Aliens," which assumes powers over alien friends not delegated by the Constitution, is not law, but is altogether void and of no force.

5. Resolved. That, in addition to the general principle, as well as the express declaration, that powers not delegated are reserved, another and more special provision inserted in the Constitution from abundant caution, has declared, "that the migration or importation of such persons as any of the States now existing shall think proper to admit, shall not be prohibited by the Congress prior to the year 1808." That this commonwealth does admit the migration of alien friends described as the subject of the said act concerning aliens; that a provision against prohibiting their migration is a provision against all acts equivalent thereto, or it would be nugatory; that to remove them, when migrated, is equivalent to a prohibition of their migration, and is, therefore, contrary to the said provision of the Constitution, and void.

6. Resolved, That the imprisonment of a person under the protection of the laws of this commonwealth, on his failure to obey the simple order of the President to depart out of the United States, as is undertaken by the said act entitled, "An Act concerning Aliens," is contrary to the Constitution, one amendment in which has provided, that "no person shall be deprived of liberty without due process of law;" and that another having provided, "that, in all criminal prosecutions, the accused shall enjoy the right of a public trial by an impartial jury,

to be informed as to the nature and cause of the accusation, to be confronted with the witnesses against him, to have compulsory process for obtaining witnesses in his favor, and to have assistance of counsel for his defence," the same act undertaking to authorize the President to remove a person out of the United States who is under the protection of the law, on his own suspicion, without jury, without public trial, without confrontation of the witnesses against him, without having witnesses in his favor, without defence, without counsel—contrary to these provisions also of the Constitution—is therefore not law, but utterly void, and of no force.

That transferring the power of judging any person who is under the protection of the laws, from the courts to the President of the United States, as is undertaken by the same act concerning aliens, is against the article of the Constitution which provides, that "the judicial power of the United States shall be vested in the courts, the judges of which shall hold their offices during good behavior," and that the said act is void for that reason also; and it is further to be noted that this transfer of judiciary power is to that magistrate of the general government who already possesses all the executive, and a qualified negative on all legislative powers.

7. Resolved, That the construction applied by the general government (as is evident by sundry of their proceedings) to those parts of the Constitution of the United States which delegate to Congress power to lay and collect taxes, duties, imposts, excises; to pay the debts, and provide for the common defence and general welfare, of the United States, and to make all laws which shall be necessary and proper for carrying into execution the powers vested by the Constitution in the government of the United States, or any department thereof, goes to the destruction of all limits prescribed to their powers by the Constitution; that words meant by the instrument to be subsidiary only to the execution of the limited powers, ought not to be so construed as themselves to give unlimited powers, nor a part to be taken as to destroy the whole residue of the instrument; that the proceedings of the general government, under color of those articles, will be a fit and necessary subject for revisal and correction at a time of greater tranquillity, while those specified in the preceding resolutions call for immediate redress.

8. Resolved, That the preceding resolutions be transmitted to the senators and representatives in Congress from this commonwealth, who are enjoined to present the same to their respective houses, and to use their best endeavors to procure, at the next session of Congress, a repeal of the aforesaid unconstitutional and obnoxious acts.

9. Resolved, lastly, That the governor of this commonwealth be, and is, authorized and requested to communicate the preceding resolutions to the legislatures of the several States, to assure them that this commonwealth considers union for special national purposes, and particularly for those specified in their late federal compact, to be friendly to the peace, happiness, and prosperity, of all the States; that, faithful to that compact, according to the plain intent and meaning in which it was understood and acceded to by the several parties, it is sincerely anxious for its preservation; that it does also believe, that, to take from the States all the powers of self-government and transfer them to a general and consolidated government, without regard to the special government, and reservations solemnly agreed to in that compact, is not for the peace, happiness, or prosperity of these States; and that, therefore, this commonwealth is determined, as it doubts not its co-States are, to submit to undelegated and consequently unlimited powers in no man, or body of men, on earth; that, if the acts before specified should stand, these conclusions would flow from them—that the general government may place any act they think proper on the list of crimes, and punish it themselves, whether enumerated or not enumerated by the Constitution as cognizable by them; that they may transfer its cognizance to the President, or any other person, who may himself be the accuser, counsel, judge, and jury, whose suspicions may be the evidence, his order the sentence, his officer the executioner, and his breast the sole record of the transaction; that a very numerous and valuable description of the inhabitants of these States, being, by this precedent, reduced, as outlaws, to absolute dominion of one man, and the barriers of the Constitution thus swept from us all, no rampart now remains against the passions and the power of a majority of Congress, to protect from a like exportation, or other grievous punishment, the minority of the same body, the legislatures, judges, governors, and counsellors of the States, nor their other peaceable inhabitants, who may venture to reclaim the constitutional rights and liberties of

the States and people, or who for other causes, good or bad, may be obnoxious to the view, or marked by the suspicions, of the President, or be thought dangerous to his or their elections, or other interests, public or personal; that the friendless alien has been selected as the safest subject of a first experiment; but the citizen will soon follow, or rather has already followed; for already has a Sedition Act marked him as a prey: That these and successive acts of the same character, unless arrested on the threshold, may tend to drive these States into revolution and blood, and will furnish new calumnies against republican governments, and new pretexts for those who wish it to be believed that man cannot be governed but by a rod of iron; that it would be a dangerous delusion were a confidence in the men of our choice to silence our fears for the safety of our rights; that confidence is everywhere the parent of despotism; free government is founded in jealousy, and not in confidence; it is jealousy, and not confidence, which prescribes limited constitutions to bind down those whom we are obliged to trust with power; that our Constitution has accordingly fixed the limits to which, and no farther, our confidence may go; and let the honest advocate of confidence read the Alien and Sedition Acts, and say if the Constitution has not been wise in fixing limits to the government it created, and whether we should be wise in destroying those limits; let him say what the government is, if it be not a tyranny, which the men of our choice have conferred on the President, and the President of our choice has assented to and accepted, over the friendly strangers, to whom the mild spirit of our country and its laws had pledged hospitality and protection; that the men of our choice have more respected the bare suspicions of the President than the solid rights of innocence, the claims of justification, the sacred force of truth, and the forms and substance of law and justice.

In questions of power, then, let no more be said of confidence in man, but bind him down from mischief by the chains of the Constitution. That this commonwealth does therefore call on its co-States for an expression of their sentiments on the acts concerning aliens, and for the punishment of certain crimes herein before specified, plainly declaring whether these acts are or are not authorized by the federal compact. And it doubts not that their sense will be so announced as to prove their attachment to limited government, whether general or particular, and that the rights and liberties of their co-States will be exposed to no dangers by remaining embarked on a common bottom with their own; but they will concur with this commonwealth in considering the said acts as so palpably against the Constitution as to amount to an undisguised declaration that the compact is not meant to be the measure of the powers of the general government, but that it will proceed in the exercise over these States of all powers whatsoever. That they will view this as seizing the rights of the States, and consolidating them in the hands of the general government, with a power assumed to bind the States, not merely in cases made federal, but in all cases whatsoever, by laws made, not with their consent, but by others against their consent; that this would be to surrender the form of government we have chosen, and live under one deriving its powers from its own will, and not from our authority; and that the co-States, recurring to their natural rights not made federal, will concur in declaring these void and of no force, and will each unite with this commonwealth in requesting their repeal at the next session of Congress.

EDMUND BULLOCK, S. H. R.

JOHN CAMPBELL, S. S. P. T.

Passed in the House of Representatives, Nov. 10, 1798.

Attest, THO'S. TODD, C. H. R.

In Senate, Nov. 13, 1798—Unanimously concurred in.

Attest, B. THURSTON, C. S.

Approved, November 19, 1798.

By the Governor,
JAMES GARRARD, Governor of Kentucky.

HARRY TOULMIN, Secretary of State.

D. The Alien and Sedition Acts

In 1798, the Federalist-controlled Congress passed a series of laws which, on the surface, were designed to control the activities of foreigners in the United States during a time of impending war. Beneath the surface, however, the real intent of these laws was to destroy Jeffersonian Republicanism. The laws, known collectively as the "Alien and Sedition Acts," included:

- The Naturalization Act, which extended the residency period from 5 to 14 years for those aliens seeking citizenship; this law was aimed at Irish and French immigrants who were often active in Republican politics.
- The Alien Act, which allowed the expulsion of aliens deemed dangerous during peacetime.
- The Alien Enemies Act, which allowed the expulsion or imprisonment of aliens deemed dangerous during wartime. This was never enforced, but it did prompt numerous Frenchmen to return home.
- The Sedition Act, which provided for fines or imprisonment for individuals who criticized the government, Congress, or president in speech or print.

Edward Livingston, in the early Congressional debate over the bills, brought out arguments similar to those that would bring down Joseph McCarthy a century and a half later:

No evidence, then, being produced, we have a right to say that none exists, and yet we are about to sanction a most important act; and on what ground? Our individual suspicions, our private fears, our overheated imaginations. Seeing nothing to excite those suspicions, and not feeling those fears, I could not give my assent to the bill even if I did not feel a superior obligation to reject it on other grounds.

"Long John" Allen of Connecticut retorted that the bill was fully justified:

> "I hope this bill will not be rejected. If ever there was a nation which required a law of this kind it is this. Let gentlemen look at certain papers printed in this city and elsewhere and ask themselves whether an unwarrantable and dangerous combination does not exist to overturn and ruin the Government by publishing the most shameless falsehoods against the Representatives of the people of all denominations, that they are hostile to free governments and genuine liberty, and of course to the welfare of this country; that they ought, therefore, to be displaced, and that the people ought to raise an insurrection against the Government."

The Alien Acts were never enforced, but the Sedition Act was. A number of Republican newspaper publishers were convicted under the terms of this law. The Jeffersonians argued quite rightly that the Sedition Act violated the terms of the First Amendment and offered a remedy in the Virginia and Kentucky Resolutions.

While these laws were either repealed or allowed to expire in the next administration, they were significant as rallying points for the Jeffersonians. The heavy-handed Federalist policies worked to the advantage of the Republicans as they prepared for the Election of 1800.

E. George Washington's Presidential Cabinet

Below is a listing of those cabinets our first president had according to our Constitution

President
Vice President
Secretary of State
Secretary of the Treasury
Secretary of War
Attorney General
Postmaster General

F. John Cornyn's Balance Budget Amendment

113th CONGRESS

1st Session

S. J. RES. 7

IN THE SENATE OF THE UNITED STATES

February 13, 2013

Mr. Cornyn (for himself, Mr. McConnell, Mr. Roberts, Mr. Hatch, Mr. Cochran, Mr. Grassley, Mr. Shelby, Mr. McCain, Mr. Inhofe, Mr. Sessions, Ms. Collins, Mr. Enzi, Mr. Crapo, Ms. Murkowski, Mr. Chambliss, Mr. Graham, Mr. Alexander, Mr. Burr, Mr. Coburn, Mr. Thune, Mr. Isakson, Mr. Vitter, Mr. Corker, Mr. Barrasso, Mr. Wicker, Mr. Johanns, Mr. Risch, Mr. Kirk, Mr. Coats, Mr. Blunt, Mr. Moran, Mr. Portman, Mr. Boozman, Mr. Toomey, Mr. Hoeven, Mr. Rubio, Mr. Johnson of Wisconsin, Mr. Paul, Mr. Lee, Ms. Ayotte, Mr. Heller, Mr. Scott, Mr. Flake, Mr. Cruz, and Mrs. Fischer) introduced the following joint resolution; which was read twice and referred to the Committee on the Judiciary

JOINT RESOLUTION

Proposing an amendment to the Constitution of the United States relative to balancing the budget.

That the following article is proposed as an amendment to the Constitution of the United States, which shall be valid to all intents and purposes as part of the Constitution when ratified by the legislatures of three-fourths of the several States:

1. Total outlays for any fiscal year shall not exceed total receipts for that fiscal year, unless two-thirds of the duly chosen and sworn Members of

each House of Congress shall provide by law for a specific excess of outlays over receipts by a roll call vote.

2. Total outlays for any fiscal year shall not exceed 18 percent of the gross domestic product of the United States for the calendar year ending before the beginning of such fiscal year, unless two-thirds of the duly chosen and sworn Members of each House of Congress shall provide by law for a specific amount in excess of such 18 percent by a roll call vote.

3. Prior to each fiscal year, the President shall transmit to the Congress a proposed budget for the United States Government for that fiscal year in which—

(1) total outlays do not exceed total receipts; and

(2) total outlays do not exceed 18 percent of the gross domestic product of the United States for the calendar year ending before the beginning of such fiscal year.

4. Any bill that imposes a new tax or increases the statutory rate of any tax or the aggregate amount of revenue may pass only by a two-thirds majority of the duly chosen and sworn Members of each House of Congress by a roll call vote. For the purpose of determining any increase in revenue under this section, there shall be excluded any increase resulting from the lowering of the statutory rate of any tax.

5. The limit on the debt of the United States shall not be increased, unless three-fifths of the duly chosen and sworn Members of each House of Congress shall provide for such an increase by a roll call vote.

6. The Congress may waive the provisions of sections 1, 2, 3, and 5 of this article for any fiscal year in which a declaration of war against a nation-State is in effect and in which a majority of the duly chosen and sworn Members of each House of Congress shall provide for a specific excess by a roll call vote.

7. The Congress may waive the provisions of sections 1, 2, 3, and 5 of this article in any fiscal year in which the United States is engaged in a

military conflict that causes an imminent and serious military threat to national security and is so declared by three-fifths of the duly chosen and sworn Members of each House of Congress by a roll call vote. Such suspension must identify and be limited to the specific excess of outlays for that fiscal year made necessary by the identified military conflict.

8. No court of the United States or of any State shall order any increase in revenue to enforce this article.

9. Total receipts shall include all receipts of the United States Government except those derived from borrowing. Total outlays shall include all outlays of the United States Government except those for repayment of debt principal.

10. The Congress shall have power to enforce and implement this article by appropriate legislation, which may rely on estimates of outlays, receipts, and gross domestic product.

11. This article shall take effect beginning with the fifth fiscal year beginning after its ratification.

G. Glossary

Abridge: To deprive; to cut off from; followed by of; as to *abridge* one of his rights, or enjoyments. to *abridge* from, is now obsolete or improper. (Webster's 1828 Dictionary)

Admiralty: In general, a court of *admiralty* is a court for the trial of causes arising on the high seas, as prize causes and the like. In the United States, there is no *admiralty* court, distinct from others; but the district courts, established in the several states by Congress, are invested with *admiralty* powers. (Webster's 1828 Dictionary)

Affirmation: A solemn declaration made under the penalties of perjury, by persons who conscientiously decline taking an oath; which *affirmation* is in law equivalent to testimony given under oath. (Webster's 1828 Dictionary)

Agency: The quality of moving or of exerting power; the state of being in action; action; operation; instrumentality; as, the *agency* of providence in the natural world. (Webster's 1828 Dictionary)

Ambassador: A minister of the highest rank employed by one prince or state, at the court of another, to manage the public concerns of his own prince or state, and representing the power and dignity of his sovereign. Embassadors are ordinary, when they reside permanently at a foreign court; or extraordinary, when they are sent on a special occasion. They are also called ministers. Envoys are ministers employed on special occasions, and are of less dignity. (Webster's 1828 Dictionary)

Amendment: A word, clause or paragraph, added or proposed to be added to a bill before a legislature. (Webster's 1828 Dictionary)

Anas: A collection of the memorable sayings of a person. (Merriam-Webster's online dictionary)

Appellate: Pertaining to appeals; having cognizance of appeals; as 'appellate jurisdiction.' (Webster's 1828 Dictionary)

Apportionment: The act of apportioning; a dividing into just proportions or shares; a dividing and assigning to each proprietor his just portion of an undivided right or property. (Webster's 1828 Dictionary)

Appropriation: 1. The act of sequestering, or assigning to a particular use or person, in exclusion of all others; application to a special use or purpose; as, of a piece of ground for a park; of a right, to one's self; or of words, to ideas.

2. In law, the severing or sequestering of a benefice to the perpetual use of a spiritual corporation, sole or aggregate, being the patron of the living. For this purpose must be obtained the king's license, the consent of the bishop and of the patron. When the *appropriation* is thus made, the appropriator and his successors become perpetual parsons of the church, and must sue and be sued in that name. (Webster's 1828 Dictionary)

Arsenal: A repository or magazine of arms and military stores, whether for land or naval service. (Webster's 1828 Dictionary)

Bill of Attainder: as used in Article I, Sections 9 and 10: Chris Trueman from the website http://www.historylearningsite.co.uk. describes it as a "piece of legislation that declared a person or persons guilty of a crime. A bill of attainder allowed for the guilty party to be punished without a trial. A bill of attainder was part of English common law. Whereas Habeus Corpus guaranteed a fair trial by jury, a bill of attainder bypassed this.

"The word 'attainder' meant tainted. A bill of attainder was mostly used for treason in England and such a move suspended a person's civil rights and guaranteed that the person would be found guilty of the crimes Stated in the bill as long as the Royal Assent was gained. For serious crimes such as treason, the result was invariably execution. The guilty person's family would find that his/

her property was confiscated by the Crown as he/she had no right to make a will. All titles held would go to the Crown. In this sense, the attainted person's family was also held to be guilty as they were also punished, though not to the same degree."

Cabinet: The select or secret council of a prince or executive government. (Webster's 1828 Dictionary)

Capitation: Numeration by the head; a numbering of persons or a tax, or imposition upon each head or person; a poll-tax. Sometimes written Capitation-tax. (Webster's 1828 Dictionary)

Census: In the United States of America, an enumeration of the inhabitants of all the States, taken by order of the Congress, to furnish the rule of apportioning the representation among the States, and the number of representatives to which each State is entitled in the Congress; also, an enumeration of the inhabitants of a State, taken by order of its legislature. (Webster's 1828 Dictionary)

Civil: Relating to the community, or to the policy and government of the citizens and subjects of a state; as in the phrases, *civil* rights, *civil* government, *civil* privileges, *civil* war, *civil* justice. It is opposed to criminal; as a *civil* suit, a suit between citizens alone; whereas a criminal process is between the state and a citizen. It is distinguished from ecclesiastical, which respects the church; and from military, which respects the army and navy. (Webster's 1828 Dictionary)

Compact: An agreement; a contract between parties; a word that may be applied, in a general sense, to any covenant or contract between individuals; but it is more generally applied to agreements between nations and states, as treaties and confederacies. So the constitution of the United States is a political contract between the States; a national *compact* Or the word is applied to the agreement of the individuals of a community. (Webster's 1828 Dictionary)

Concur: To agree; to join or unite, as in one action or opinion; to meet, mind with mind; as, the two houses of parliament *concur* in the measure. (Webster's 1828 Dictionary)

Concurrent: Joint and equal; existing together and operating on the same objects. The courts of the United States, and those of the States have, in some cases, *concurrent* jurisdiction. (Webster's 1828 Dictionary)

Confederation: The act of confederating; a league; a compact for mutual support; alliance; particularly of princes, nations or states. The United States of America are sometimes called the *confederation*. (Webster's 1828 Dictionary)

Consul: In modern usage, the name *consul* is given to a person commissioned by a king or state to reside in a foreign country as an agent or representative, to protect the rights, commerce, merchants and seamen of the state, and to aid the government in any commercial transactions with such foreign country. (Webster's 1828 Dictionary)

Elector: One who elects, or one who has the right of choice; a person who has, by law or constitution, the right of voting for an officer, In free governments, the people or such of them as possess certain qualifications of age, character and property, are the electors of their representatives, etc., in parliament, assembly, or other legislative body. In the United States, certain persons are appointed or chosen to be electors of the president or chief magistrate. (Webster's 1828 Dictionary)

Emolument: The profit arising from office or employment; that which is received as a compensation for services, or which is annexed to the possession of office, as salary, feels and perquisites. (Webster's 1828 Dictionary)

Enumerate: To count or tell, number by number; to reckon or mention a number of things, each separately; as, to *enumerate* the stars in a constellation; to *enumerate* particular acts of kindness; we cannot *enumerate* our daily mercies. (Webster's 1828 Dictionary)

Excise: An inland duty or impost, laid on commodities consumed, or on the retail, which is the last state before consumption; as an *excise* on coffee, soap, candles, which a person consumes in his family.

But many articles are excised at the manufactories, as spirit at the distillery, printed silks and linens at the printer's, etc. (Webster's 1828 Dictionary)

Export: To carry out; but appropriately, and perhaps exclusively, to convey or transport, in traffic, produce and goods from one country to another, or from one state or jurisdiction to another, either by water or land. We *export* wares and merchandize from the United States to Europe. The Northern States *export* manufactures to South Carolina and Georgia. Goods are exported from Persia to Syria and Egypt on camels. (Webster's 1828 Dictionary)

Ex Post Facto: as used in Article I, Sections 9 and 10 retroactively criminalizes conduct which was not criminal when it was done.

Example: You barbequed outside last Sunday and that it was lawful when you did it. Next month, Congress makes a law which purports to retroactively criminalize barbequing outdoors. What you did is a crime for which you are subject to criminal prosecution, even though when you did it, there was no crime.

Democracy: Government by the people; a form of government, in which the supreme power is lodged in the hands of the people collectively, or in which the people exercise the powers of legislation. Such was the government of Athens. (Webster's 1828 Dictionary)

Federal: Consisting in a compact between parties, particularly and chiefly between states or nations; founded on alliance by contract or mutual agreement; as a *federal* government, such as that of the United States. (Webster's 1828 Dictionary)

Alternate: A federation of sovereign States united under a national government only for those limited purposes itemized in the Constitution, with all other powers reserved by the States or the People. (Publius Huldah)

Habeas Corpus: A writ of habeas corpus is a judicial mandate to a prison official ordering that an inmate be brought to the court so it can be determined whether or not that person is imprisoned lawfully and whether or not he should be released from custody. (Lectlaw.com)

Impeach: To accuse; to charge with a crime or misdemeanor; but appropriately, to exhibit charges of maladministration against a public officer before a competent tribunal, that is, to send or put on, to load. The word is now restricted to accusations made by authority; as, to *impeach* a judge. (Webster's 1828 Dictionary)

Imposts: Any tax or tribute imposed by authority; particularly, a duty or tax laid by government on goods imported, and paid or secured by the importer at the time of importation. Imposts are also called customs. (Webster's 1828 Dictionary)

Infringe: To break, as contracts; to violate, either positively by contravention, or negatively by non-fulfillment or neglect of performance. A prince or a private person infringes an agreement or covenant by neglecting to perform its conditions, as well as by doing what is stipulated not to be done. (Webster's 1828 Dictionary)

Invasion: A hostile entrance into the possessions of another; particularly, the entrance of a hostile army into a country for the purpose of conquest or plunder, or the attack of a military force. An attack on the rights of another; infringement or violation. (Webster's 1828 Dictionary)

Laws of Nations: The rules that regulate the mutual intercourse of nations or states. These rules depend on natural law, or the principles of justice which spring from the social state; or they are founded on customs, compacts, treaties, leagues and agreements between independent communities. (Webster's 1828 Dictionary)

Legislature: the body of men in a state or kingdom, invested with power to make and repeal laws; the supreme power of a state. The *legislature* of Great Britain consists of the house of lords and the house of commons with the king, whose sanction is necessary to every bill before it becomes a law. The legislatures of most of the states in America, consist of two houses or branches, but the sanction of the govenor is required to give their acts the force of law, or a concurrence of two thirds of the two houses, after he has declined and assigned his objections. (Webster's 1828 Dictionary)

Letter of Marque: Letters of reprisal; a license or extraordinary commission granted by a sovereign of one state to his subjects, to make reprisals at sea on the subjects of another, under pretense of indemnification for injuries received. *marque* is said to be from the same root as marches, limits, frontiers, and literally to denote a license to pass the limits of a jurisdiction on land, for the purpose of obtaining satisfaction for theft by seizing the property of the subjects of a foreign nation. I can give no better account of the origin of this word. (Webster's 1828 Dictionary)

Letter of Reprisal: A commission granted by the supreme authority of a state to a subject, empowering him to pass the frontiers [marque,] that is, enter an enemy's territories and capture the goods and persons of the enemy, in return for goods or persons taken by him. (Webster's 1828 Dictionary)

Liberty: Natural *liberty* consists in the power of acting as one thinks fit, without any restraint or control, except from the laws of nature. It is a state of exemption from the control of others, and from positive laws and the institutions of social life. This *liberty* is abridged by the establishment of government. (Webster's 1828 Dictionary)

Magazine: A store of arms, ammunition or provisions; or the building in which such store is deposited. It is usually a public store or storehouse. In ships of war, a close room in the hold, where the gunpowder is kept. Large ships have usually two magazines. (Webster's 1828 Dictionary)

Magna Charta: Written document, presented on June 15, 1215 in England that recognized certain liberties and legal procedures. It contained sixty-three chapters and established the beginnings of trial by jury, due process, Habeas Corpus, and equality under the law. (Thefreedictionary.com)

Militia: The body of soldiers in a state enrolled for discipline, but not engaged in actual service except in emergencies; as distinguished from regular troops, whose sole occupation is war or military service. The *militia* of a country are the able bodied men organized into companies, regiments and brigades, with officers of all grades, and required by law to attend military exercises on certain days only, but at other times left to pursue their usual occupations. (Webster's 1828 Dictionary)

Misdemeanor: Ill behavior; evil conduct; fault; mismanagement. In law, an offense of a less atrocious nature than a crime. Crimes and misdemeanors are mere synonymous terms; but in common usage, the word crime is made to denote offenses of a deeper and more atrocious dye, while small faults and omissions of less consequence are comprised under the gentler name of misdemeanors. (Webster's 1828 Dictionary)

Naturalization: The act of investing an alien with the rights and privileges of a native subject or citizen. *naturalization* in Great Britain is only by act of parliament. In the United States, it is by act of Congress, vesting certain tribunals with the power. (Webster's 1828 Dictionary)

Perjury: The act or crime of willfully making a false oath, when lawfully administered; or a crime committed when a lawful oath is administered in some judicial proceeding, to a person who swears willfully, absolutely and falsely in a matter material to the issue.

Pursuant: Done in consequence or prosecution of anything; hence, agreeable; conformable. *pursuant* to a former resolution the house proceeded to appoint the standing committees. This measure was adopted *pursuant* to a former order. (Webster's 1828 Dictionary)

Republic: A commonwealth; a state in which the exercise of the sovereign power is lodged in representatives elected by the people. In modern usage, it differs from a democracy or democratic state, in which the people exercise the powers of sovereignty in person.

Yet the democracies of Greece are often called republics. (Webster's 1828 Dictionary)

Rule of Law: Adherence to due process; government by law. (Merriam-Webster's online dictionary)

Rule of Man: The absence of rule of law. It is a society in which one person or a group of persons rule arbitrarily. (Wikipedia)

Treason: In the United States, *treason* is confined to the actual levying of war against the United States, or in adhering to their enemies, giving them aid and comfort. (Webster's 1828 Dictionary)

Treaty: An agreement, league or contract between two or more nations or sovereigns, formally signed by commissioners properly authorized, and solemnly ratified by the several sovereigns or the supreme power of each state. Treaties are of various kinds, as treaties for regulating commercial intercourse, treaties of alliance, offensive and defensive, treaties for hiring troops, treaties of peace, etc. (Webster's 1828 Dictionary)

Tribunal: Properly, the seat of a judge; the bench on which a judge and his associates sit for administering justice. More generally, a court of justice; as, the house of lords in England is the highest *tribunal* in the kingdom. (Webster's 1828 Dictionary)

Usurpation: The act of seizing or occupying and enjoying the property of another, without right; as the *usurpation* of a throne; the *usurpation* of the supreme power. (Webster's 1828 Dictionary)

Vested: Fixed; not in a state of contingency or suspension; as *vested* rights. (Webster's 1828 Dictionary)

Veto: A forbidding; prohibition; or the right of forbidding; applied to the right of a king or other magistrate or officer to withhold his assent to the enactment of a law, or the passing of a decree. (Webster's 1828 Dictionary)

Welfare: Exemption from any unusual evil or calamity; the enjoyment of peace and prosperity, or the ordinary blessings of society and civil government. (Webster's 1828 Dictionary)

Writ: That which is written. In this sense, *writ* is particularly applied to the Scriptures, or books of the Old Testament and New Testament; as holy writ; sacred *writ* . (Webster's 1828 Dictionary)

H. Acknowledgments

The below listed folks were great assistance in getting this book to you, dear reader.

My wife, Marilyn Hilliard
Daughter, Suzi Hilliard
Frank Kuchar
Daughter and Son-in-Law, Karen and Chris Byer
Daughter and Son-in-Law, Jill and Kenny Allison
Granddaughter Emily Byer
Grandsons Jake Byer and Austin Collins

Teacher panel:

Geraldine Ivey
Nancy Coppock
Bill Hunter
Marilyn Hilliard

Other assistance
provided by:

Shawn and Geraldine Ivey
Margaret Henson
Lucie and Kelly Dowe
Kay and Doc Clauson
Jim Lewis
Jerry Koch

42922319R00139

Made in the USA
Middletown, DE
25 April 2017